VOLUME 1

GENESIS

Linda B. Hinton

ABINGDON PRESS
Nashville

GENESIS

Copyright © 1988 by Graded Press

All rights reserved.

This book is printed on recycled, acid-free paper.

Library of Congress Cataloging-in-Publication Data

Cokesbury basic Bible commentary.
  Basic Bible commentary/by Linda B. Hinton . . . [et al.].
    p. cm.
  Originally published: Cokesbury basic Bible commentary. Nashville:
  Graded Press © 1988.
  ISBN 0-687-02620-2 (pbk.: v.1: alk. paper)
    1. Bible—Commentaries.   I. Hinton, Linda B.   II. Title.
  [BS491.2.C65   1994]
  220.7—dc20

94-10965
CIP

ISBN 0-687-02620-2 (v. 1, Genesis)
ISBN 0-687-02621-0 (v. 2, Exodus–Leviticus)
ISBN 0-687-02622-9 (v. 3, Numbers–Deuteronomy)
ISBN 0-687-02623-7 (v. 4, Joshua–Ruth)
ISBN 0-687-02624-5 (v. 5, 1–2 Samuel)
ISBN 0-687-02625-3 (v. 6, 1–2 Kings)
ISBN 0-687-02626-1 (v. 7, 1–2 Chronicles)
ISBN 0-687-02627-X (v. 8, Ezra–Esther)
ISBN 0-687-02628-8 (v. 9, Job)
ISBN 0-687-02629-6 (v. 10, Psalms)
ISBN 0-687-02630-X (v. 11, Proverbs–Song of Solomon)
ISBN 0-687-02631-8 (v. 12, Isaiah)
ISBN 0-687-02632-6 (v. 13, Jeremiah–Lamentations)
ISBN 0-687-02633-4 (v. 14, Ezekiel–Daniel)
ISBN 0-687-02634-2 (v. 15, Hosea–Jonah)
ISBN 0-687-02635-0 (v. 16, Micah–Malachi)
ISBN 0-687-02636-9 (v. 17, Matthew)
ISBN 0-687-02637-7 (v. 18, Mark)
ISBN 0-687-02638-5 (v. 19, Luke)
ISBN 0-687-02639-3 (v. 20, John)
ISBN 0-687-02640-7 (v. 21, Acts)
ISBN 0-687-02642-3 (v. 22, Romans)
ISBN 0-687-02643-1 (v. 23, 1–2 Corinthians)
ISBN 0-687-02644-X (v. 24, Galatians–Ephesians)
ISBN 0-687-02645-8 (v. 25, Philippians–2 Thessalonians)
ISBN 0-687-02646-6 (v. 26, 1 Timothy–Philemon)
ISBN 0-687-02647-4 (v. 27, Hebrews)
ISBN 0-687-02648-2 (v. 28, James–Jude)
ISBN 0-687-02649-0 (v. 29, Revelation)
ISBN 0-687-02650-4 (complete set of 29 vols.)

00 01 02 03—10 9 8 7 6 5 4

MANUFACTURED IN THE UNITED STATES OF AMERICA

Contents

Outline of Genesis

12. Isaac and Ishmael (21:1-21)
13. Abraham's covenant with Abimelech (21:22-34)
14. God tests Abraham (22:1-24)
15. The death of Sarah (23:1-20)
16. Isaac and Rebekah (24:1-67)
17. The death of Abraham (25:1-18)
B. Isaac, Jacob, and Esau (25:19–27:46)
  1. Birth and rivalry of Jacob and Esau (25:19-34)
  2. The blessings of Isaac (26:1-35)
  3. Jacob receives Isaac's blessing (27:1-46)
C. Jacob in exile (28:1–31:55)
  1. Jacob's dream at Bethel (28:1-22)
  2. Jacob, Leah, and Rachel (29:1–30:24)
  3. Jacob and Laban (30:25–31:55)
D. Jacob in Canaan (32:1–35:29)
  1. Jacob wrestles with "a man" (32:1-32)
  2. Jacob and Esau are reconciled (33:1-20)
  3. Shechem and Dinah (34:1-31)
  4. Jacob comes to Mamre (35:1-29)
E. The descendants of Esau (36:1-43)
III. The Story of Joseph (37:1–50:26)
A. Joseph sold into slavery (37:1-36)
B. Judah and Tamar (38:1-30)
C. Joseph in Egypt (39:1–50:26)
  1. Trials and successes (39:1–41:57)
  2. Joseph's family in Egypt (42:1–45:28)
  3. Jacob's migration to Egypt (46:1–47:31)
  4. Jacob's death (48:1–50:14)
  5. Joseph's last years (50:15-26)

Introduction to Genesis

The book of Genesis is a book about how the universe, the earth and its creatures, faith, and the community of faith all began. At its heart, however, Genesis is a statement of faith. The stories in this book testify that all reality begins with God and that nothing exists except by the will and power of God. These stories tell us that, if we push each question of "Why?" or "How?" about our world to its ultimate end, the answer must be: God.

The book of Genesis is also about relationships. From "the beginning" relationships are established between God and creation and among the different parts of creation. No part exists in isolation. The relationship that receives the most attention in Genesis is the relationship between God and the community of faith. This community was born in the relationship established between God and Abraham, and it continues to this day.

Title, Date, and Authorship

The Hebrew title of Genesis comes from the first word in the text, which means "in the beginning (of)," and the name Genesis comes from the Septuagint title (the oldest Greek translation of the Old Testament). Genesis is part of the Pentateuch, the first five books of the Old Testament, which is also called the Torah ("law"). These books are traditionally referred to as the "five books of Moses." The close association of Moses with the law and the specific records he did write (see, for example, Exodus 17:14) have helped to foster the idea that Moses wrote the Pentateuch. Most scholars agree, however, that Moses was not the author of the Pentateuch. Indeed, there is much evidence within the books themselves that more than one person contributed to them.

The sources and writers of the Pentateuch, and of Genesis in particular, are still the objects of much study and debate. There are, however, some generally accepted opinions about how the books came about:

(1) Before much of the material in these books was written it was preserved in oral form. This is the "oral tradition," the stories, history, laws, prayers, and poems that were passed from one generation to the next before they were written down and collected.

(2) Four sources of this tradition are found in the Pentateuch. Each source has a characteristic style, language, and perspective that (in many cases) allow it to be identified. There is no definite agreement concerning which parts of the Scripture belong to which source, and some commentators find more than four sources within the text.

(3) The four most widely accepted sources are called J, E, P, and D. "J" gets its name from the characteristic use of *Yahweh* (Jehovah) as the name for God in this source. "E" uses the name *Elohim* (divine being) for God. "P" stands for "priestly" because much of the material from this source focuses on the interests of priests and on the sanctuary. "D" stands for Deuteronomy and is associated with much of the material in the book of Deuteronomy. J, E, and P are found in the book of Genesis.

(4) The writers who put together each of these sources probably used both oral and written material, much of which was ancient even in their day. Exact dates for J, E, P, and D are not known, nor do we know exactly when the book of Genesis was put into the form we know today. Estimates have been made, however, about the general dates for these sources. J perhaps took shape during the reigns of King David and King Solomon

(1000–922 B.C.), E may have developed during the eighth century B.C., P may come from the time of the exile (587–539 B.C.) or soon after, and D in its earliest form probably comes from approximately 650 B.C.

(5) Some scholars believe that one person collected these various sources (and other material, for example, from *The Book of the Wars of the LORD*, Numbers 21:14) and formed them into the books we have today. Others believe that the collection and formation was done over a number of years by more than one person.

(6) Genesis and the other books of the Pentateuch were put together sometime during or after the Jewish exile in Babylon (587–539 B.C.). The process of writing and organizing the text may have continued for a long time, but the process was completed before 250 B.C. when the Septuagint translation of the Old Testament was begun.

The Content of Genesis

The content of Genesis can be divided into three broad sections: the primeval history (Creation through the tower of Babel), the patriarchal history (Abraham, Isaac, and Jacob), and the story of Joseph.

Each of these sections is a collection of different kinds of materials such as stories, genealogical lists, prayers, and poems. The biggest part of Genesis is taken up with stories about particular people in specific circumstances and times. These stories, however, also have an application and a point beyond the individual lives involved. Genesis is like a "family history" for the community of faith.

Though we use the word *history* in relation to the events described in Genesis, we do not mean history in our modern sense of the word. The writers of Genesis did not produce objective, footnoted, cross-referenced documents with specific dates for the people and events they describe. They had a very definite perspective from which they wrote the book, and this perspective is that all reality, and specifically the reality of the community of faith, is grounded in the will and power of God. They wrote a theological history that seeks to preserve the experiences, remembrances, and beliefs of this earliest community.

This is not to say, however, that what they wrote is not true or historical. The trend of archaeological and other historical research in recent years has been to illuminate more fully this ancient world and to confirm the scriptural account. To be sure, many questions remain unanswered, and, to our twentieth-century minds hungry for facts on which to base our beliefs, there may never be enough answers. The writers of Genesis, however, are calling us beyond this issue to larger questions that they do indeed answer: How did this world come to be? What is our place in the world? How did the community of faith begin?

THE EARLY HEBREWS' IDEA OF THE UNIVERSE (See *Job 11:7-8*)

Illustration from *International Lesson Annual 1961*, copyright
© 1960, by Abingdon Press, used by permission.

The Genealogies in Genesis 4–5

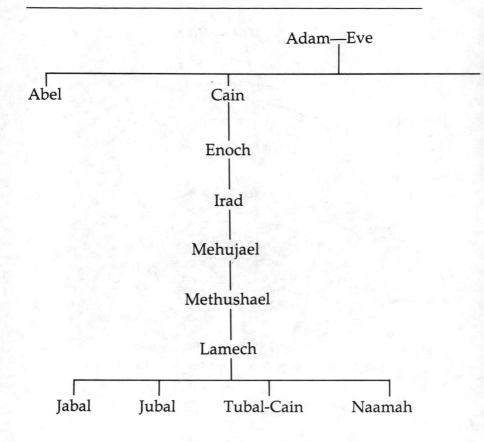

Adam—Eve

Abel   Cain

Enoch

Irad

Mehujael

Methushael

Lamech

Jabal   Jubal   Tubal-Cain   Naamah

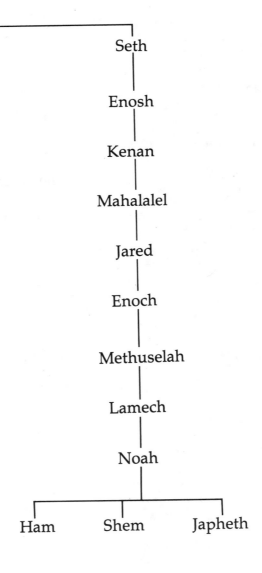

Seth

Enosh

Kenan

Mahalalel

Jared

Enoch

Methuselah

Lamech

Noah

Ham   Shem   Japheth

The Covenants in Genesis

With Noah   Genesis 9:8-17

With Abraham   Genesis 12:1-3

                                   Genesis 15:18-21

                                   Genesis 17:9-14

                                   Genesis 22:15-18

With Isaac   Genesis 26:2-5

With Jacob   Genesis 28:13-15

PART ONE Genesis 1

Introduction to This Chapter

Genesis 1:1–2:4*a* is the story of Creation as told in the priestly (P) tradition (see the Introduction on pages 7-10). This story is told in stately, rhythmical, and dignified language and is similar to a liturgy that might be used in a worship service.

This account is based, to some extent, on the "science" of its day that assumed that the universe is divided into three parts: the heavens, the earth, and the underworld. This story of Creation also has some similarities to accounts of Creation from other cultures in the ancient Near East, particularly that of Mesopotamia. Genesis 1, however, goes beyond any ancient or modern scientific or cultural explanation for Creation. The writer declares that everything, all reality, depends on the sovereign will and power of God for its existence. Nothing is independent or self-sustaining, but all is dependent upon the Creator.

Here is an outline of this section.
 I. From the Beginning to the First Day (1:1-5)
 II. The Second Day (1:6-8)
 III. The Third Day (1:9-13)
 IV. The Fourth Day (1:14-19)
 V. The Fifth Day (1:20-23)
 VI. The Sixth Day (1:24-31)
 VII. The Seventh Day (2:1-4*a*)

From the Beginning to the First Day (1:1-5)

The New International Version translation says, *In the beginning God created the heavens and the earth. Now the earth was formless and empty.* The New Revised Standard Version puts it slightly differently: *In the beginning when God created the heavens and the earth, the earth was a formless void.* Both translations testify that the earth was at first in a state of chaos, a "formless waste" that was created and then further acted upon by God. Thus God moves to bring order and purpose out of waste and chaos.

Creation does not come out of nothing; it comes out of God. Before Creation there was God. Because of God's will and word (*and God said*) there is the created order of the universe.

Verses 3-5 describe God's creation of light and separation of it from the darkness. This light is not dependent upon the sun, moon, or stars, which have not yet been created (see verses 14-19). The heavenly bodies carry light and establish the rhythm of day and night, but they are not the source of light. God is the source. The writers of Genesis 1 also know that life on earth depends upon light, so the creation of light must come before the creation of life on earth.

That the light is *good* means that it is pleasing to God; it conforms to God's will. The Hebrew day begins at sundown, so the *evening* and the *morning* in that order mark the first day. This refrain ends each account of the six days of God's creative activity (see also verses 8, 13, 19, 23, 31).

The Second Day (1:6-8)

The Hebrew word that is translated *dome* (NRSV) or *expanse* (NIV) refers to something that is beaten out, or stamped, like metal. This image reflects the ancient view that the sky is a solid dome that is stretched over the earth (see, for example, Job 37:18; Psalm 104:2-3). This dome holds back the waters above the heavens and keeps them from overwhelming the earth. The waters under the dome include the water on the earth and the water under the earth.

In the Old Testament, water is seen as a gift from God that is essential for life. People need water for themselves and their crops, and it is a means of physical and ritual cleansing. Water can also represent the forces of chaos, as it does in this part of the Creation story. The *waters* and the *deep* are part of creation, but they must be kept under God's control. God's decree holding back the waters allows the work of creation on earth to continue.

God *calls* or names each part of creation as part of the process of bringing it into existence (see also Psalm 33:9).

The Third Day (1:9-13)

The third day is marked by two acts of creation. The dry land appears as the waters on and underneath the earth are held back and gathered together. This sets the stage for the next act of creation in which vegetation appears. The original plants and trees are given the power to reproduce themselves through their seeds.

The Fourth Day (1:14-19)

Light has been in existence since the first day of Creation. Now God makes the sun, moon, and stars as particular sources of light. In ancient times many people worshiped the heavenly bodies as gods or goddesses. This account of Creation makes clear that heavenly bodies are not divine and have no power in and of themselves. The sun and moon do not *rule* (NRSV) or *govern* (NIV) in the sense of gods, but are the dominant sources of light for day and night that are under God's control.

In very practical terms, lights in the sky also serve as markers by which people can measure time: days, seasons, and years.

The Fifth Day (1:20-23)

All of creation up until now has been affirmed as good; now it is also blessed. The living creatures of the water and air are created and receive the first blessing of creation from God (verse 22). This blessing shows that, though creation is not to be complete without humankind, the rest of creation is of value to God and is in relationship with God.

The Sixth Day (1:24-31)

This day also contains two major acts of creation.

In verses 24-25 the land animals are created—both domestic and wild animals as well as insects and reptiles.

Verses 26-27 describe God's creation of humankind *in our image*; after creating them God gives them special duties. The plural *our* may refer to God alone as an indication of divine majesty (especially since verse 27 uses the singular *his*). *Our* may also refer to a heavenly council or court with which God talks over this significant part of the creation process.

Image and *likeness* refer to the same thing: "the likeness of our image." The context for understanding what this means may be found in a common practice of biblical times. When a ruler could not be physically present in all of his territory, he put up an image of himself in outlying provinces of his empire as evidence of his dominion over them. The people acknowledged this image as proof of his rule.

Of course, a living person is not the same as a lifeless image, but the principle of representation is similar. God creates human beings as representative likenesses of the Creator. This likeness is physical to some extent because, in this life at least, the body is part of being a whole person. This likeness is also spiritual, emotional, and intellectual—human beings share (to a limited extent) God's power to think, feel, and act. Human beings are an emblem or standard by which God's lordship over creation is to be recognized. This image is both male and female (verse 27) and is not complete without both.

Human beings are told to *rule* (NIV) or *have dominion* (NRSV) over the other living creatures on the earth. This means that people are to act on God's behalf as stewards of creation. As representatives (images) of God, human beings are given the responsibility of seeing that God's will for creation is fulfilled. God's purposes, not human purposes, set the standard by which dominion is defined.

God's blessing to humankind is also a command (verses 28-31). They, like the other creatures, are to reproduce themselves. They are to *subdue* or master the earth in order to produce food for themselves. This does not mean they are to treat creation in any way they want to. Rather, people are to act as God's stewards toward the earth and the living creatures so that the bounty and fruitfulness of the earth is continued.

Both people and animals are to be vegetarians, eating only seeds and plants (verses 29-30).

The Seventh Day (2:1-4*a*)

God celebrates the completion of Creation by resting on the seventh day. This seventh day becomes the sabbath (*to cease*). The people of Israel originally celebrated the sabbath as a day of rest rather than as a day of worship. For human beings, the practice of a day of rest (now in combination with worship) is a recognition that the existence of the world does not depend upon our efforts. The created order depends upon God for its existence. We are to rest in imitation of God and in recognition that life is a gift.

The *generations* (NRSV verse 4*a*) refer to the *account* (NIV) or story of the creation of heaven and earth.

§ § § § § § §

The Message of Genesis 1

The people who put together the book of Genesis and those who arranged the Bible realized that the testimony of Genesis 1 is the ground upon which everything else in the Bible builds. It is appropriate that the witness of the community of faith should open with "the beginning."

What does Genesis 1 tell us about how the world was created and for what purpose?

§ Old Testament tradition declares that God's wisdom and God's word existed before Creation and are the means of Creation. The prologue to the Gospel of John (John 1:1-18) affirms this and declares that Christ is the wisdom and word behind Creation.

§ The act of creation belongs to God alone. The verb "to create" that is used in Genesis 1 is applied only to God, never to anything or anyone else.

§ Creation is a concrete expression of God's will.

§ All creation is unified under and obedient to God's will. This is the established order that God pronounces as "good."

§ This "good" not only conforms with God's will but is also beautiful and pleasing.

§ Human beings, who are created in the image of God, are entrusted with dominion on earth as God's representatives in God's service. The greatest example of such service is found in the life of Jesus, who, as the *image of God* (2 Corinthians 4:4) came to serve humankind and creation.

§ Human beings and the rest of creation are not divine but are sacred and are blessed.

§ § § § § § §

Genesis 2–3

Introduction to These Chapters

This story of Creation comes from the Yahwist (also called "J"; see the Introduction). J's account of Creation focuses on the first human beings and explores their relationship to God.

Here is an outline of Genesis 2–3.
I. The Garden and the First Living Being (2:4b-17)
II. The Creation of Woman (2:18-24)
III. A Choice Is Made (3:1-13)
IV. Consequences of the Choice (3:14-24)

The Garden and the First Living Being (2:4b-17)

In verses 4b-7, the LORD God (*Yahweh Elohim*) makes the heavens, the earth, and humankind. The Lord God forms man (Hebrew, *adam*) from the dust or clods of the ground (Hebrew, *adamah*) as a potter forms a vessel from clay. The Hebrew name for *man* (which means humankind) is closely related to the word for *ground*. This is not just a play on words, but is a way of expressing the fundamental connection between humankind and the earth.

The man's physical self is then animated by God's breath and he becomes a *living being* or a living soul. The Hebrew word for breath means a puff of wind or of vital breath. This word can also refer to divine inspiration. The word for soul comes from the Hebrew root word *to breathe.* A soul is a living creature. Thus, the breath of life gives the creature made from dirt a new quality; the "man of dust" becomes a complete person.

The word *Eden* (verse 8) may be based on a Sumerian word that means *plain* or *steppe.* The word is also similar to the Hebrew noun meaning *enjoyment.* The exact location of Eden is unknown. It has traditionally been located somewhere in Mesopotamia, which is east of Canaan.

The *tree of life* is a tree whose fruit preserves life. The *tree of the knowledge of good and evil* is a tree whose fruit gives divine knowledge (see Genesis 3:22).

The four streams or rivers associated with Eden (verses 10-14) cannot be identified exactly except for the Tigris and the Euphrates (see the Glossary). The Pishon is said to flow around the land of Havilah, which may be part of Arabia. The Gihon flows around the land of Cush, which in this case probably does not mean Ethiopia. This Cush may be the land of the Kassites that extends eastward from Babylonia. These rivers are believed to converge somewhere near the head of what is now called the Persian or Arabian Gulf. Ancient traditions among the people there place the garden of Eden in the marshy, fertile area at the head of the gulf.

In verses 15-17, God places the man in the garden with specific duties and instructions. The man is given a vocation: He is entrusted with the garden and is to see to its fruitfulness by tilling the ground and tending the trees. The man is given permission to take his sustenance from the garden. The man is also given limits to his domain: He is not to eat from the tree of the knowledge of good and evil, for when he eats it he will be sentenced to death.

Even in paradise there are limits, and the human creature is expected to respect these limits. Since it makes no sense to give an order to someone who is incapable of either keeping it or breaking it, the man must have the capacity for obedience or disobedience from the beginning. He must know, to some extent, the difference between right and wrong, good and evil.

What kind of knowledge then does the tree of the knowledge of good and evil give? In the Old Testament, knowledge involves comprehension but it also involves the will. Events and actions (either divine or human) are also knowledge. Thus, we have knowledge not only in what we think but in what we do.

In the Old Testament, what is "good" is defined by God: God and God's laws are good. This good is not only moral and religious but also includes what is beautiful, practical, and useful in life. "Evil" is what is contrary to God's laws—what is bad, wicked, injurious, or corrupt. Thoughts or actions and their consequences can be good or evil. Thus, "good and evil" covers the whole range of possibilities in human existence.

Choosing to eat of the fruit of the tree of the knowledge of good and evil is evil because it is against God's law. By choosing evil, humankind will know not only the good they experience in the garden but also the whole range of evil possibilities in life.

The Creation of Woman (2:18-24)

God seeks a *helper* for the man. Though elsewhere in Scripture God is called a *helper* for humankind (see, for example, Isaiah 41:10), the man also needs another creature alongside him, one who corresponds to him. The Hebrew word for *helper* comes from two root words, one that means "to surround" (that is, to protect or save) and one that means "to be strong." Such a creature is found when God makes a woman and brings her to the man.

The man immediately recognizes her as part of himself and as a kindred soul. In the man's poem of recognition (verse 23) the man and woman are first called *man* (Hebrew, *ish*) and *woman* (Hebrew, *ishshah*). With the creation of the woman, humankind is complete.

In verse 24 the writer of this story adds a comment on the marriage customs that result from the way man and woman are created for one another. The man and woman no longer look to parents as their primary companions and helpers in life. The husband-wife relationship is primary. They are *one flesh* physically and spiritually.

The man and woman are at ease with their created selves; they feel no shame at being naked. In the Old Testament, shame comes from being conscious of one's guilt, unworthiness, or failure. To be put to shame is to be disgraced. The man and woman live unashamed before each other and before God because, as yet, they have no sense of guilt or failure.

A Choice Is Made (3:1-13)

The *serpent* is the most shrewd and cunning of all the creatures God made. The serpent is not Satan or a symbol of evil or of death. He is a creature of God who introduces to humankind the possibility of disobedience to God's will.

In verses 1-5 the serpent asks the woman a question that is a distortion of God's command in 2:16-17. The woman corrects the serpent but adds something that God did not say, a prohibition of touching the fruit. The serpent then accuses God of lying and of wanting to keep Godlike power away from the humans.

In verse 6 the woman listens to the serpent and then considers the tree. Its fruit looks savory; the tree is beautiful and is to be coveted as a source of wisdom. The ability to know good from evil does not seem to be the point of the rule against eating the fruit of this tree. The man and woman are expected to know that eating from the tree is wrong, and they are expected to choose to obey God's law. Instead, the woman decides to satisfy her appetite, curiosity, and desire for power.

That wisdom is related to power is evident in the Old Testament's treatment of wisdom in general. Wisdom is seen as a way to master life and its problems. Ideally, wisdom leads not only to an ability to handle the world but also to self-mastery. Wisdom is often seen as a gift from God, and to have wisdom is believed to be a worthy desire. What the woman and the man fail to consider in deciding to eat of the tree is that *the fear of the LORD* is the beginning of knowledge (Proverbs 1:7). Of course, this proverb is not explicitly stated in this story, but the principle applies: The first priority in gaining wisdom is a respect for and awareness of one's proper place in relation to God. The man and woman are unwilling to accept the limits of God's created order. They are free to choose, and they choose more knowledge over more trust.

In verse 7, the Hebrew word rendered *knew* (NRSV) or *realized* (NIV) also means *to experience,* or *to come to know.* To know in the sense desired by the woman and the man, then, is to be in full possession of mental and physical powers. What they get instead is shame. They see themselves in a new light and they don't like what they see.

Modern psychology tells us that shame is a "master emotion" that influences all our other emotions. Shame arises from a sense of failure and brings with it self-loathing and feelings of unworthiness. Shame, thus, affects our basic sense of self and is experienced most often as embarrassment or humiliation. Shame is a normal feeling in some circumstances but it can become harmful when it controls our basic ideas about who we are or how worthy we are.

Knowledge from the fruit of the tree brings shame (verse 7) and fear (verse 10). The man and woman experience these feelings even before God confronts them with their disobedience. Choosing to be disobedient gives them knowledge, but it is a knowledge of failure and of unworthiness. This is not knowledge that, as the devious serpent had promised, is to be desired. They are embarrassed about their bodies and are afraid of God.

According to verses 8-13, another result of their new knowledge is fear of God because they know they have done wrong and feel guilty for it. The man and the woman, in trying to defend themselves from responsibility for their disobedience, distance themselves from one another and from God. The man tries to place the final blame on God, who created the woman. The woman tries to blame the serpent. Instead of harmony and oneness between Creator and creation there is now shame, anxiety, and alienation.

Consequences of the Choice (3:14-24)

The serpent, for his part, is condemned to a life of lowliness, crawling in the dust, and of hostility with humans.

The woman is condemned to bear her children in pain. She will still desire her husband, for together they create children, but their relationship has changed. They were created to live together in oneness of flesh and spirit. Because of their disobedience, they now live in a broken relationship that is expressed in her pain and in his ruling over her.

The man will continue to till and tend the earth as he has done in the garden, but this work will become toil. There will be antagonism between the man and the ground, just as there will be between the serpent and humans and between the man and the woman. The harmony of God's original creation has been broken.

The story does not make clear whether the man and woman are created mortal or immortal. God says in verse 19 that the fate of humankind is to return to the ground in death, just as was promised in Genesis 2:17. This seems to imply that death is the result of disobedience to God's law. On the other hand, God sends the man and woman out of the garden to keep them from eating of the tree of life (that was in the garden from the beginning, see 2:9) and becoming immortal (verses 22-23). This implies that they are created mortal.

The Hebrew word for *Eve* (verse 20) is similar to the word for *living*. She is to be blessed with children and honored as the mother of humankind.

The clothes that God makes for Adam and Eve are a symbol of God's protective care. God's power and care go with them. Though their relationship to God is damaged, it is not destroyed.

God says the man and woman have become *like one of us* (verse 22), like divine beings (perhaps referring to the heavenly council). They are now capable of thinking about and experiencing the full range of human possibilities—both good and evil—but they will not gain immortality. Immortality will be no substitute for life in the garden. The *cherubim* guard against any further access to the garden or to the tree of life. Humankind must live with the consequences of disobedience.

§ § § § § § §

The Message of Genesis 2–3

The story of Creation in Genesis 2–3 focuses on the place of human beings in God's created order. Human beings are not created in isolation but are made to live in communion with the earth and its creatures, with one another, and with God. What does this story tell us about the relationship between the Creator and humankind?

§ Human beings are created to live in harmonious relationship with God, with one another, and with the rest of creation.

§ Human beings are created with the capacity to understand and obey God's laws.

§ Human beings are given a vocation and are given limits on how they may use God's creation. These limits, if respected, will lead to well-being.

§ Fear, anxiety, and shame come from a failure to trust God and to obey the limits that God sets for human existence.

§ Sin is related to the desire of humans to grasp the power of God.

§ Brokenness in creation is related to human sin. This brokenness includes the alienation that exists among people and between people and God.

§ There is no freedom or security for humankind apart from God.

§ § § § § § §

PART THREE Genesis 4:1–6:4

Introduction to These Chapters

The story of humankind continues outside the garden of Eden. This part of the story explores how the relationship of human beings to one another affects their relationship to God.

These chapters may be outlined as follows.
  I. Cain and Abel (4:1-16)
  II. Family of Cain and the Birth of Seth (4:17-26)
  III. From Adam to Noah (5:1-32)
  IV. The Nephilim (6:1-4)

Cain and Abel (4:1-16)

In verses 1-2, Eve gives birth to two sons with God's help, that is, through God's benevolent providence. Abel grows up to be a shepherd, and Cain becomes a farmer like his father. Some interpreters see the traditional longstanding conflicts between nomads and settlers reflected in this story of conflict between Cain and Abel, though the story itself does not emphasize this issue.

According to verses 3-7, people have now begun to formally worship God by bringing offerings from the products of their labor. No explanation is given for God's rejecting Cain's offering. Perhaps Cain does not bring the firstlings or best of his produce to God, though Abel brings the fattest of his flock. For whatever reason, God pays heed to Abel's offering but not to Cain's.

God responds to Cain's anger at this situation with a series of questions and a declaration (verses 6-7). God declares that Cain, despite being born and raised outside of paradise, can still *do well* (NRSV) or *do what is right* (NIV). That is, he can live faithfully before God, and thus be accepted by God.

God then says that *sin* (alienation from God) is like a predatory animal that lies in wait for Cain when he chooses to not live faithfully. Sin, however, can be mastered. The Hebrew verb translated as *must master* (verse 7) means more than any one English translation is able to show. This verb may also be translated "can master," "shall master," or "may master." Thus, God's statement to Cain about mastering sin is a command, an invitation, and a promise.

In verses 8-12, rather than trusting God and mastering sin, Cain kills his brother. When God confronts him with the crime, Cain denies responsibility for anything beyond his own needs.

Cain has polluted the ground that is supposed to provide his sustenance, and the ground testifies against him. Blood is believed to be the source of bodily vitality and power. Shedding innocent blood (bloodguilt) defiles both the murderer and the land.

Because of his crime, Cain is now at odds with the earth. No longer will the earth yield its fruits (NRSV = *strength*) for his sustenance. He will become a fugitive, a wanderer.

According to verses 13-16 Cain is driven from his home, from his vocation as a farmer, and from God's benevolent presence. The *mark* of Cain is perhaps like a tattoo. This mark brands Cain with his guilt, but it is also a signal of God's mercy and protection of him.

The land of Nod is the land of "wandering."

Family of Cain and the Birth of Seth (4:17-26)

The writers of this story do not say who Cain's wife is or where she is from. God may have created other people after the creation of Cain's parents, or, the creation of humankind as described in Genesis 1:26-27 may indicate that more than one pair of male and female human beings are created on the sixth day (just as more than two of each kind of animal are created).

Cain does not wander all his life but founds a city, probably somewhere in Mesopotamia. The "song of the sword" (verses 23-24) is a tribal song of vengeance. The violence among humankind that was begun by Cain is increased tenfold by his descendants.

Verses 25-26 describe a new line of descent from Adam and Eve beginning with the birth of Seth. Worship of God (calling upon or invoking *the name of the* LORD) is also begun anew. Offerings to God (as begun by Cain and Abel) also continue. Now, however, people invoke the Lord by name. God later reveals the divine name to Moses (see Exodus 3:13-15; 6:2-3). In addition to this personal revelation, however, the writer of Genesis 4:26 testifies that God's relationship with humankind has not faltered. God is participating in the human story and is known by this new family.

From Adam to Noah (5:1-32)

This genealogical list is from the priestly historian (see the Introduction) and covers the time in human history from Creation to the Flood. Ten generations are named to show the line of humankind from its creation *in the likeness of God* to the sorry state humankind reaches in the time of Noah. This list serves both as a conclusion to the story of Adam's family and an introduction to the story of Noah. Since in the Old Testament the number ten is often used to symbolize completion, these ten generations may represent the completion of this age or stage in human history.

The life span of human beings gradually declines until the limit of one hundred and twenty years is reached (see

Genesis 6:3). Seventy or eighty years is more common (see Psalm 90:10).

The Hebrew name *Noah* (verse 29) means *rest* or comfort under God's blessing. Through Noah, the broken relationship between humankind and the ground will be restored. People will still have their God-given vocation of tilling and tending the earth, but their labor need not be toil and they need not work in vain.

The Nephilim (6:1-4)

This story tells about the origins of the Nephilim and about the limit to human life set by God. The exact meaning of the word *Nephilim* is not known, but these people are apparently a giant race (see also Numbers 13:33) thought to descend from the union of divine beings and human beings. Other ancient cultures also have stories about such unions and the children they produce.

These divine beings are "immortal" as compared to the human "mortals," and this union of mortal with immortal is a perversion of the order of Creation. Because of this God moves to limit the years of human beings and their mortal/immortal cousins to a hundred and twenty years. The life span of humans gradually declines (see Genesis 5:1-31), and after this only three people (Abraham, Isaac, and Jacob) live longer than a hundred and twenty years.

Thus, God once again establishes control over the *spirit* or breath of life. This story leads into the story of the Flood, in that God also acts to regain control over the earth and its inhabitants.

§ § § § § § §

The Message of Genesis 4:1–6:4

The stories of Adam, Eve, Cain, and Abel tell us that these persons are not only our physical ancestors but our spiritual ancestors as well. We can see ourselves in them and learn more about our relationship to God through their stories.

The stories in Genesis 4–6 testify that God is both judge and redeemer. What do these chapters tell us about sinful humankind's relationship to this God who both condemns and protects?

§ The story of Cain and Abel shows us that our relationships with one another affect our relationship to God. We cannot be false to each other without also being false to God.

§ We can, may, and shall master sin. We are created to "do well" before God, but this requires great effort and constant diligence. Sin is an intimate enemy who resides on our doorstep and seeks us out.

§ We and the earth suffer the consequences of our sin.

§ God controls the spirit or breath of life and moves to assert this control whenever human or divine beings overstep their limits.

§ Despite human sin, God has not given up on creation. God is in relationship to humankind and is available to those who call upon the name of the Lord.

§ § § § § § §

Genesis 6–9

Introduction to These Chapters

Genesis 6:5–9:29 tells the story of the great Flood and of God's covenant with Noah following the Flood. (Note: The first four verses of chapter 6 were treated in Part Three.) Noah is remembered and honored in the Bible as a man of uncommon righteousness whose obedience to God saved humankind from complete destruction (see also Ezekiel 14:14, 20; Hebrews 11:7).

The story of the Flood as it stands today in the text is a combination of ancient Israelite traditions. The historians P and J (see the Introduction on pages 7-10) both contributed material to this final version. Other ancient cultures (for example, the Sumerians of Mesopotamia and natives of North America) also have stories of a great world flood that few human beings survived.

Despite some similarities between the Mesopotamian stories and the Israelite stories, however, one major difference stands out. In the Mesopotamian versions (such as the Babylonian *Gilgamesh Epic*), the flood comes seemingly at the whim of the gods and humankind survives only through the pity of one god. In the Israelite version, both the Flood and the survival of humankind are by the will and power of God, the Lord of Creation.

Here is an outline of Genesis 6–9.
   I. Reasons for the Flood (6:5-8)
  II. Preparations for the Flood (6:9–7:10)

Reasons for the Flood (6:5-8)

God regrets creating people, because they are thoroughly wicked. The heart is the center of a person's character, and the thoughts and plans of the heart reflect a person's beliefs, attitudes, and desires. People have so contaminated the earth with their sin that God decides to destroy not only people but the other living creatures as well.

The basis for God's judgment and planned destruction is the extent to which God's original intentions in Creation have been thwarted. There is almost universal brokenness between Creator and creation. The Hebrew word in verse 7 that tells of God's grief at this situation (*I am sorry* [NRSV] *grieved* [NIV]) is the same word used in Genesis 3:16 to tell of Eve's pain in childbearing. Both God and people are paying a price for human sin.

Preparations for the Flood (6:9–7:10)

Among all the lawless and corrupt people of the earth in that age, Noah and his sons are found to be righteous and blameless. To be righteous is to be in right relationship with God and to live according to God's commands. To be blameless is to be found without reproach in this relationship.

The case that God makes against humankind shows God's righteousness as well. The coming destruction is not motivated by malice or by whim but has its basis in God's justice. God, as the sole Creator and Lord of all, acts to reclaim and redeem the creation. God's justice, however, includes both judgment and mercy.

The exact identity of *cypress wood* (verse 14) is

unknown, though it is perhaps some type of conifer.
Pitch is a hydrocarbon mixture that is similar to asphalt
and is used to waterproof the ark. Even today, boats
constructed of reeds and covered with pitch are used for
transportation by people living in the marshes at the
head of the Persian Gulf.

The ark is 450 feet long by 75 feet wide by 45 feet high.
Similar large ships with more than one deck are known
to have been used in Mesopotamia and in Egypt in
ancient times.

The two traditions out of which this story was written
are evident in 6:17–7:5. Verses 17-22 are from P; 7:1-5 is
from J. Each tradition tells of God's intentions to save
Noah's family (verses 18 and 7:1), and each tells what
they are to take with them on the ark (verses 19-21 and
7:2-3). Note the differences in the number of animals
Noah is instructed to take. Whatever the number saved,
it was obviously sufficient!

The people and animals are still vegetarian (see also
later instructions in 9:4).

Clean and *unclean* refer to ritual purity (see, for
example, the laws in Leviticus 11).

The Flood (7:11-24)

The waters above the firmament and the waters below
the earth (see Genesis 1:6-10) are loosed upon the earth
for forty days and nights. The number forty is often used
in the Bible to signify a long, complete, or appropriate
period of time.

Evidence of a great flood in ancient times, which
included most of the known world at that time, has been
found in Mesopotamia. Archaeologists have found a
layer of mud from ten to thirteen feet thick, like that
which is deposited by water, under the ruins of the
Sumerian city of Ur in Mesopotamia. Under the mud are
the ruins of an even older city.

All in whom there is the merest breath of life are

blotted out from the face of the earth, except for those in the ark.

Dry Land Appears (8:1-19)

To *remember* (see verse 1) is not just a mental activity. Remembering also involves action. God's remembrance of Noah brings God's grace, mercy, and action on Noah's behalf.

Olive trees (verse 11) do not grow at high elevations, so the olive leaf plucked by the dove shows that the waters have drained away from the low-lying areas as well as from the mountains.

As the people and animals leave the ark God issues a command and blessing like that of Creation, *be fruitful* and *multiply* (compare Genesis 1:22, 28). Life on earth has been cleansed and given a new start.

Offering and Promise (8:20-22)

Noah sacrifices some of the animals from the ark in worship and thanksgiving to God. God accepts this offering and makes a remarkable promise. Despite the fact that the flood has not changed human nature—people still devise evil—God will never again doom the earth and its creatures to complete destruction. As long as the earth itself lasts, the natural cycles initiated at Creation will endure.

Noah and his family carry the seeds of hope for the future, for humankind to make a fresh and obedient start in God's creation. They also, however, carry the capacity for evil and for disobedience.

Blessing and Covenant (9:1-17)

Verses 1-7: Noah and his family receive God's blessing and command to *be fruitful and grow in numbers* (compare Genesis 1:28). They are placed in a dominant relationship with the other living creatures of the earth and are given permission to eat meat as well as vegetables and grains (compare Genesis 1:29-30).

Human beings are given boundaries, however. The blood of a human or animal is a sign of life (see also the comments on Genesis 4:8-11), and all life belongs to and is dependent upon God. Therefore, people must not consume the blood (life). Murder, the shedding of innocent blood, is also forbidden. Since human beings are created in God's image (see the comments on Genesis 1:26), to murder the image of God is also to strike at God. (In Israelite law, animals are also held accountable for murder; see Exodus 21:28-29.)

Verses 8-16: Through Noah and his sons God makes a covenant for all time with all humanity and the other living creatures of the earth. God takes the initiative and is the one solely responsible for maintaining the terms of the covenant.

Verses 8-11: At its most basic, a covenant is an agreement between two parties. Some covenants place requirements on each of the partners (see, for example, Genesis 12:1-3). God's covenant with Noah, however, requires only God's maintenance and remembrance. Despite the disruptions in God's original intentions for creation and despite the grief and trouble humanity has caused for God, God decides not to abandon the creation.

There will certainly be evil in the world because there will be people in the world (see 8:21). But God promises never again to deal with this evil by sending a flood to destroy the earth. The watery forces of chaos will be held in check.

Verses 12-16: To some ancient peoples, rainbows were a sign of war. They believed that rainbows were the heavenly bows from which the gods shot lightning bolts. God, however, intends the rainbow to be a sign of grace and mercy. The bow is to remind both humanity and God of the promises God makes to Noah's family. God remembers the promises made and maintains an eternal commitment to creation (see also the comments on 8:1). The bow is also a reminder to humanity of God's lordship and mercy.

The Curse of Canaan (9:18-29)

This is a story about culture and politics as well as about familial and tribal relationships. The story shows that the evil imaginations of the hearts of human beings (see 8:21) continue to affect the course of human history.

Noah settles down to an agricultural life, fulfilling the vocation given to humankind by God at Creation (see Genesis 2:5, 15). The culture of vines and the making of wine is traced to Noah, as are the consequences of overindulging in fruit of the vine. (Drinking of wine is itself not condemned in the Bible, but the sins to which overindulgence can lead are condemned.)

The exposure of one's genitals is considered shameful and degrading. Though Ham may have unwittingly seen Noah's exposure, telling his brothers (instead of perhaps covering his father and saying nothing) brings on Noah's curse.

The action in this story is somewhat confusing because it is Ham who is said to see his father's nakedness, but it is Ham's son, Canaan, who bears Noah's curse. Noah's curse, however, shows that Canaan represents not just an individual but also a nation. Verse 19 says that the world is peopled from Noah's sons and the Canaanites are one of the peoples to come from Ham and Canaan (see also 10:15-20).

The Israelites had to struggle throughout much of their history against the influence of Canaanite religion and morality (see, for example, the laws of Leviticus 18:6-18, 24-30). The origin of Canaanite perversions and excesses are traced to Ham and Canaan, their common ancestors. According to Noah's curse, they are destined to serve the peoples descended from Shem (who eventually include the Israelites) and from Japheth (who share the land with Shem's descendants). This is not a curse on a race of people but on an nation/individual who is said to act dishonorably and shamefully.

§ § § § § § §

The Message of Genesis 6–9

The story of the flood and its aftermath clearly shows that human sin and the capacity of humankind for evil continue to affect human history. What does this story tell us about the relationship between human history and human sin?

§ Human sin and the capacity of humankind for evil continue to affect human history because sin affects the relationship between humankind and God.

§ A fundamental witness in the community of faith is that God judges and is active in human history. Creation has not just been turned loose to work out its own destiny.

§ God acts in human history to accomplish the righteous purposes for which the world was created.

§ Human sin affects the course by which these righteous purposes are achieved, but sin will not ultimately block God's purposes.

§ God's judgment is mixed with grace.

§ Humankind owes its existence to God's grace, not to its own merit.

§ § § § § § §

Genesis 10–11

Introduction to These Chapters

Genesis 10–11 begins with an overview of how the world's families spread from Noah's family and divided themselves into distinct peoples (10:1–11:9). Attention is then focused on the family of Abraham, through which will come the Israelite people (11:10-32).

Here is an outline of these chapters.
  I. The Descendants of Noah (10:1-32)
 II. The Tower of Babel (11:1-9)
III. The Descendants of Shem to Abram (11:10-32)

The Descendants of Noah (10:1-32)

This chapter, often called the Table of Nations, summarizes the ancestry of the nations known in the world at the time Genesis was written. This summary contains information from both the P and J historians (see the Introduction). This list is said to organize the peoples of the world by families, languages, lands, and nations (see verse 20), though political and geographic divisions are predominant.

Verses 2-5: Sons (NIV) means *descendants* (NRSV), as these lists contain not only individual names but also the plural names of ethnic groups (for example, *Kittim*). The descendants of Japheth settle north of Mesopotamia and westward into the coastal areas of the eastern

Mediterranean. These areas include Media, Lydia, Greece, and Cyprus.

Verses 6-20: The descendants of Ham settle in northeast Africa and in Canaan. The name *Cush* is used in the Bible to indicate two different lands. In verse 6 it means an area in modern Ethiopia; in verses 8-12 it means the land of the Kassites in Mesopotamia. *Put* is probably in modern Libya. The Canaanites settle on the coast of Palestine in what will become Phoenicia and in central and southern Palestine. They are connected geographically and politically with their relatives in northeastern Africa.

Verses 8-12: This account of Nimrod's greatness refers to the Mesopotamian Cush rather than the African Cush. Nimrod is a mighty conqueror *before* God (that is, by the will of God, or simply, on earth). He founds a great kingdom in the land of Sumer (*Shinar*, later called Babylonia), builds many great cities, and is credited as the founder of the Assyrian and Babylonian civilizations.

Verses 21-32: The descendants of Shem, the elder brother of Japheth, include peoples of Assyria, Aram, and Arabia. Elam is included as a next-door neighbor to the east of Mesopotamia.

The children of Eber are the Hebrews, which include the Israelites through Eber's son, Peleg. Peleg's descendants are listed in Genesis 11:18-26, which introduces Abraham with whom the Israelite people begin.

The name *Peleg* has been explained as a play on words using the Hebrew word *divide*. That the world was divided during Peleg's lifetime may refer to the Tower of Babel story (see Genesis 11:1-9) or to the fact that he and his brother, Joktan, began the two main branches of the Semitic peoples, which include Israel. Joktan's descendants are the Arabian peoples; Peleg's descendants include the peoples of Mesopotamia and Aram.

The Tower of Babel (11:1-9)

The setting of this story is the land of Sumer (*Shinar*) in Mesopotamia. It has been compared to a Babylonian story about the beginnings of the city of Babylon. In the pagan story, the builders of Babylon take great pride in constructing a sacred building with its head raised toward the sky.

In contrast, the biblical account of the building of the city and tower is critical of the builders and tells of the confusion that results from their efforts to reach the heavens.

Verses 1-4: This episode probably takes place before the scattering of peoples described in chapter 10. People migrating into the Tigris-Euphrates basin decide to cooperate in building a city where they may settle and a tower that will give them access to the heavens. To *make a name* for oneself means to be renowned, to have an enduring name. To have a name also means to have a reputation, either for good or bad. If the builders of the city have a reputation as a powerful people, then they can resist the forces that may scatter them and cause them to leave their new home.

The resistance to being scattered, however, is in conflict with God's command to fill the earth (see Genesis 1:28; 9:1).

Verses 5-9: God confounds the builders' plans by confusing their language. That is, various groups come to speak different languages, and they can no longer understand or listen to one another. This confusion disrupts their unity and their plans for seeking fame and security. Their desire for self-assured security, not God-directed security, leads them into confusion and dispersion.

The name *Babel* is similar to the Hebrew word for confusion.

The Descendants of Shem to Abram (11:10-32)

Information from the book of generations (see Genesis 5:1) is continued here with a special emphasis on the family into which Abraham is born.

This passage leads into what are called the *Patriarchal Narratives* (Genesis 12–36) of the Old Testament. Abraham and his family probably lived sometime around 1800-1750 B.C., and with them the biblical narrative moves from primeval times into the time of recorded history.

Though no documents outside the Bible have been found that tell about the patriarchs specifically, much has been discovered about the world in which Abraham's family moved. Personal names and place names like some listed in these verses have been found in the documents of other peoples in Mesopotamia and Palestine at this time. The historical and social settings of the patriarchal stories are in agreement with what is known from archaeological discoveries about the lands and peoples among whom the patriarchs lived. Thus, the biblical narrative takes a turn here from the dimly-seen reaches of the past into the increasing light of historical affirmation.

Verses 27-30: Terah's home is identified as *Ur of the Chaldeans*. Ur was an important port and religious center on the Euphrates River in southern Sumeria (though some scholars identify the Ur associated with Abraham with a district in northern Mesopotamia). A ziggurat, or stepped pyramid, built in Ur some 4,000 years ago, still stands today, though the river has changed its course and no longer runs by the ruins of the once-great city. The term *Chaldeans* is a later name for Babylonia that is used here to identify this part of Mesopotamia.

The statement in verse 30 that Sarah is barren anticipates the mystery and power of God's remarkable call to Abraham in 12:1-3, and it highlights Abraham's obedient response.

Verses 31-32: The story does not say why Terah and his family leave Ur for Canaan. Beginning around 2000 B.C. and continuing throughout the patriarchal age, Mesopotamia went through an extended period of political and military instability with the breakup of the once-great Sumerian culture. There were also some widespread shifts in population in Mesopotamia during this time as desert tribes from Arabia moved into the more fertile areas. Terah's move may be motivated, in part, by this situation.

Terah's family may be city-dwellers, or they may be herdsmen from the north who are not permanent residents of the city. In any case, they leave Ur and follow the well-traveled routes along the Euphrates River to the northwest. These trade routes connect Mesopotamia and Egypt by following the Fertile Crescent along the Tigris-Euphrates basin, down through Syria and Canaan, then across to Egypt. Terah and his family reach Haran, in what is now southern Turkey, and settle there. At this time, Haran is a busy, cosmopolitan trading city at the intersection of two major caravan routes, one east-west and one north-south. It is here that God calls Abraham on to Canaan.

§ § § § § § §

The Message of Genesis 10–11

The genealogies of Genesis 10–11 serve as a bridge between the primeval time in human history and what we call historical time. These family lists also serve as a bridge between the peoples of the world at large and the family of Israel in particular. The historians of Genesis leave no doubt that all the families of the earth are interrelated. They also indicate that something special is about to happen with this one particular family, and thus, set the stage for God's call of Abraham. With this call, the pessimism of Genesis 11:1-9 is tempered with hope. In the midst of the confusion and alienation of humankind, God selects a particular people, a particular man with whom to initiate a special relationship. What do these chapters tell us about the continuing relationship between God and humankind?

§ All peoples and nations owe their existence to God's grace and God's plans for creation.

§ All begin with God's blessing and promise.

§ Even so, people still seek equality with God (compare the "fruit of tree of knowledge" story in Genesis 2–3 with the story of the Tower of Babel).

§ Despite human presumption and disobedience, God's purposes will not be thwarted.

§ In the midst of a universal movement away from the Creator, God acts to create a people through whom God's original intentions for creation may be realized.

§ § § § § § §

Genesis 12

Introduction to This Chapter

This chapter is a turning point in the narrative of the book of Genesis. The story of the human family in Genesis has gradually narrowed its focus from all the world's families (Genesis 10:1-32), to one particular family (Genesis 11:10-32), then to one particular man (12:1).

Chapter 12 has two main parts.
  I. God Calls Abraham (12:1-9)
 II. Abraham and Sarah in Egypt (12:10-20)

God Calls Abraham (12:1-9)

God calls Abram (which means *exalted father*, later named *Abraham*—see Genesis 17:5) to be in a special relationship with God. No reason is given for this call. Abraham is identified only as an old, childless man in the family established by Shem, Noah's eldest son. The reasons that Abraham is chosen lie in the mystery of God's wisdom and grace, and any merit Abraham may have as a person who is particularly responsive to God is evident only later. Nevertheless, Abraham (*father of a multitude*) is to become the founding father of the nation of Israel and the spiritual father of Judaism, Christianity, and Islam.

Verses 1-3: God's call to Abraham can be divided into two main parts: what Abraham must do (verse 1), and what God will do (verses 2-3). For his part, Abraham must break his traditional ties to his homeland and family. He must look for his security in God rather than in the time-honored ways in which he has grown up. God calls him to risk and to trust.

In return, God promises Abraham descendants who will be a great nation. The word *nation* means not just a group of people but also a territory, a base of power, a homeland. *Blessing* is God's free and gracious giving of the means to fullness of life. To be blessed is to experience this fullness, which includes family, well-being, honor, wisdom, and faith.

In accepting this new relationship with God, Abraham will become a source of blessing for other people. To *bless* another person is to pass on the blessings that one has received from God. To *curse* someone is to intend harm to him or her and to resist the blessing that God bestows.

The last part of verse 3 can be translated *and by you all the families of the earth shall bless themselves* or *in you all the families of the earth shall be blessed*. This statement may be interpreted, on the one hand, to mean that present and future generations may look to Abraham as their model for blessed living as followers of the one true God. On the other hand, this promise also encompasses the blessing that will come to the world through the nation Abraham will found and through his descendant, Jesus Christ.

Notice that as soon as God has narrowed the focus of attention from all of the world to one man, the focus is expanded again. This one man is called to God's purposes not merely for his sake but also for the sake of *all the families of the earth* (NRSV; NIV = *all peoples on earth*).

Verses 4-9: Abraham, his nephew Lot, their families, and their servants leave Haran and travel through Syria and the Transjordan, choosing a route that will provide grass and water for their flocks. God appears to Abraham at his camp near Shechem to confirm that this is the land that is meant for him and his descendants. Abraham responds by building an altar in thanksgiving to God and as a memorial to the great promise made on this spot. By building an altar he also acknowledges God's claim on the land in his behalf despite the fact that the land is occupied by the Canaanites.

The exact spot where Abraham camps between Bethel and Ai is not known. Here he builds another altar to worship God and to claim the land as God's own. He calls on God's name, which carries God's power and identity. To call on the holy name is to acknowledge God's lordship as well as to offer thanksgiving, praise, and petition to God.

Abraham and Sarah in Egypt (12:10-20)

Abraham's faith in God's promises is tested, and he fails. God, however, remains true to the promises and to the divine purposes to which Abraham and Sarai have been called.

Verses 10-13: Abraham and his family abandon the Promised Land because of famine. They trust in the Egyptian breadbasket rather than in God's providence. Once there, Abraham again abandons God's promises in order to save his own skin by allowing Sarai to be identified as his sister (see also Genesis 20:12).

Verses 14-20: The promise that Abraham and Sarai will give birth to a great nation is put in jeopardy when Sarai almost becomes one of Pharaoh's wives. Abraham's faithless action brings God's curses on Pharaoh, who somehow is wise enough to understand the situation.

§ § § § § § §

The Message of Genesis 12

Abraham and his family leave Egypt richer than when they came, though not out of merit or faithfulness. Only God's intervention and faithfulness to the divine promises save the family that will one day become the people of Israel.

What does this chapter tell us about God and about humankind, represented by Abraham?

§ God does not necessarily choose perfect people to fulfill God's purposes in the world.

§ Abraham is both faithful and faithless. He is the father not only of all who believe in God but also of all who sometimes fail in belief and in trust.

§ God acts to keep the divine promises and purposes alive.

§ § § § § § §

PART SEVEN Genesis 13–15

Introduction to These Chapters

Abraham returns to the Promised Land where his journey of faith continues. These chapters may be divided into three main parts.

I. Abraham and Lot Part Ways (13:1-18)
II. War with the Kings of the East (14:1-24)
III. God's Covenant with Abraham (15:1-21)

Abraham and Lot Part Ways (13:1-18)

Abraham and Lot agree to respect one another's territorial rights, and Abraham providentially receives the land designated by God for his descendants.

Verses 1-13: The prosperity that Abraham and Lot enjoy eventually leads to a conflict over space, since they are not alone in the land but must share it with Canaanites and Perizzites. Lot chooses the greener pastures of the Jordan valley but also must live among wicked, sinful people (which leads to dire consequences for his family; see chapter 19).

Abraham, in generously letting Lot choose, receives the better part. He trusts God to provide for his needs, for his family, and for his flocks.

Verses 14-18: The hill country around Bethel is at the heart of what will become the nation of Israel. From these hills, Abraham can see large portions of the land of Canaan. God's invitation to look at this land is also an invitation for Abraham to claim it for himself and for his innumerable descendants.

Abraham responds to God's invitation and promise by settling at Hebron and building another altar to God (see also the comments on Genesis 12:4-9 concerning altars). Hebron is in the hill country southeast of Jerusalem and is in an area suited for the cultivation of vineyards as well as for the pasturing of flocks along the edges of the Judean desert to the east.

The *oaks of Mamre* (NRSV; NIV = *great trees*) are a grove of trees in the forested hills near Hebron, which perhaps belong to an Amorite named Mamre (see Genesis 14:13).

War with the Kings of the East (14:1-24)

This chapter tells of Abraham's involvement in a war between an alliance of kings from the east and an alliance of kings from the region of the Dead Sea. The material in this chapter may have been adapted by the historians of Genesis from non-Israelite records to which they had access. In this account, Abraham is shown as a powerful chieftain who commands a significant fighting force and who enjoys the respect of his pagan neighbors.

Verses 1-12: The exact identities of the kings named here remain unknown. The two alliances are perhaps fighting over access to trade routes between Egypt and southern Arabia, or perhaps over rights to the copper mines south of the Dead Sea. Lot and his family become part of the spoils of war for the victorious kings from the east.

Verses 13-16: The identification of Abraham as *the Hebrew* is interesting because, elsewhere in the Bible, Israelites are not called Hebrews except by non-Israelites or by Israelites who are identifying themselves to an outsider. The use of this title here lends support to the idea that this material originally comes from a non-Israelite historical source.

Abraham commands a force of fighters who were born

in his house. They may be high-ranking, trusted slaves who were born into service to Abraham's family rather than having been purchased. The Amorites living near Abraham who are his allies also join the expedition (see verse 24).

Verses 17-20: The king of Sodom and the king of Jerusalem (then called *Salem*) meet Abraham in the King's Valley near Jerusalem. Melchizedek, the king of Jerusalem, is also a Canaanite priest. In the name of his god, *God Most High*, he blesses Abraham and offers thanksgiving for Abraham's success. This God Most High is the high god of the Canaanite religion of that day.

A similar title, *Most High God*, is later applied to God by the people of Israel (see, for example, Daniel 5:18; 7:18) who honor God as the true maker of heaven and earth.

The *tenth* that Abram gives Melchizedek is not a religious offering but is a standard payment to one in authority. At this time, the territory in which Abraham lives may owe political allegiance to the king in Jerusalem.

Verses 21-24: Abraham apparently has captured goods and people in his successful raid. He refuses the offer of a share in this bounty by affirming his allegiance to *the* Lord, *God Most High*. This title refers to God, even though it is similar to the name in verse 19. Abram declares that he will not be obligated to the king of Sodom by taking any of the captured goods. His obligations are to God.

God's Covenant with Abraham (15:1-21)

This chapter tells of God's promises to Abraham concerning an heir (verses 1-5) and a homeland (verse 7), and the covenant that God makes with Abraham to ratify these promises (verses 8-11, 17-21).

Verses 1-6: God appears to Abraham with words of comfort and assurance, but Abraham confronts God with the fact that, despite past promises, he and Sarah remain childless. Though God may command him to *fear not,* Abraham is afraid and discouraged. By ancient law, a slave can be adopted as an heir to a childless couple, and Abraham is beginning to believe that this will be his fate.

In response, God offers Abraham no new evidence that the promised heir will come. Rather, God challenges Abraham to renewed faith by repeating the promise and giving Abraham an illustration of just how abundantly the promise will be fulfilled (see also Genesis 13:16). The stars are also a sign to Abraham that God's promises are valid. Every night the heavenly lights will also be a reminder to him of these promises.

Abraham puts his trust in the Lord, who reckons it to his merit or righteousness. To be righteous (in right relationship with God) is to trust God's promises and purposes, even against so-called common sense or reason.

Verses 7-11: God gives Abraham a guarantee that the Promised Land will really be his. This guarantee is in the form of a covenant by which God is bound to keep the promises to Abraham about his land and his descendants.

A covenant is a solemn agreement between two parties that is sealed with an oath and (sometimes) by symbolic actions. In the Old Testament there are covenants between people (see, for example, Genesis 31:43-49), between individuals and God (see, for example, 2 Samuel 23:1-7), and between a people (Israel) and God (see, for example, Deuteronomy 5:1-2). In some covenants both partners commit themselves to certain obligations; in others only one partner is formally committed to the agreed conditions.

God's covenant with Abraham is one in which God makes all the covenant promises (compare Deuteronomy 5:32-33). Abraham's only (unspoken) obligations are trust and righteousness (see verse 6), and he must provide the animals that are sacrificed in the covenant ceremony.

An ancient expression for covenant making is to "cut" a covenant, which perhaps relates to the cutting of sacrificial animals in the covenant ceremony. The shed blood of the animals may symbolize the blood relationship or kinship that the covenant establishes between the partners.

Verses 12-16: In the midst of the covenant ceremony God speaks to Abraham about Israel's future slavery in Egypt and about the Exodus. Abraham feels the darkness and dread that these times will bring. These verses offer an explanation for the delay in the fulfillment of the covenant promises. Abraham may live to a happy old age, secure in the knowledge that, though the promises will be delayed for generations, they will be fulfilled.

The Amorites, like the Canaanites, are peoples living in Canaan when Abraham and his family arrive there. They are destined to give up their land to Israel because of their sins, but the time is not yet at hand (see also Genesis 9:25-27).

Verses 17-21: The smoke and fire symbolize God's presence that passes between the pieces of the sacrifice to ratify the covenant.

The boundaries of the Promised Land are the river or brook of Egypt on the Sinai peninsula and the Euphrates River in Syria. The nation of Israel controlled all of this territory during the reigns of David and Solomon (see 2 Samuel 8:3; 1 Kings 4:21).

§ § § § § § §

The Message of Genesis 13–15

Abraham is remembered by later generations as a man of extraordinary faith (see, for example, Hebrews 11:8, 17). What does Abraham's life tell us about living a life of faith?

§ Abraham is not a man of perfect faith, but God chooses him anyway and does not give up on him even in his moments of doubt.

§ God brings Abraham outside his tent (Genesis 15:5) and forces him to see another perspective on his situation. God is the Lord of the universe, the one who made and set the stars in their places. The vastness of God's power is offered in contrast to the smallness of Abraham's trust. God challenges Abraham to expand his vision.

§ Abraham responds to God's challenge with trust (Genesis 15:6). By this we know that trust is essential to righteousness, to merit before God.

§ To be in covenant with God requires patience as well as trust. This covenant relationship also requires a recognition that real security lies not in kings or goods or in the best pastures, but in God.

§ Acceptance of God's promises requires not only trust but also an external response. Abraham moved to Hebron, built an altar, turned down the reward from the King of Sodom, and participated in the covenant ceremony. He put his faith and trust in God into action.

§ § § § § § §

Genesis 16–18

Introduction to These Chapters

These chapters tell of more waiting and more
frustration for Abraham and Sarah and of God's
continued assurances that the great promises made so
many years before will come true. They may be outlined
as follows.

    I. Hagar and Ishmael (16:1-16)
   II. The Covenant of Circumcision (17:1-27)
 III. Promises and Punishment (18:1-33)
       A. Promises and laughter (18:1-15)
       B. Intercession for Sodom and Gomorrah (18:16-33)

Hagar and Ishmael (16:1-16)

Ten years after Abraham and Sarah settle in the
Promised Land and after God promises Abraham
descendants as numerous as *the dust of the earth* (see
Genesis 13:16), Abraham and Sarah still have no children.
Sarah decides that God is not going to send the promised
heir, so she takes matters into her own hands.

Verses 1-6: Sarah is within her legal rights to secure a
substitute to bear a child for her by Abraham. Other
ancient cultures had such provisions in their legal codes.
Under the law, the wife is to retain the first and
controlling place in the relationship and is to have
authority over the child who is born to her husband and
the concubine. If the concubine seeks to take the wife's

place, the wife may demote her to her former status as a slave but may not sell her.

Sarah and Abraham, though legally correct, act against God's intentions and promises. This brings them only strife and ill-will. Sarah may not get rid of the offending Hagar, but she does abuse her and makes her life so unbearable that Hagar runs away.

Verses 7-16: God intervenes both on behalf of Hagar and her child and on behalf of the purposes God has for Abraham and Sarah. Hagar will not die in the wilderness, and her child will have many descendants. The child, however, will not take the place of the heir intended for Abraham and Sarah.

The *angel* is the Lord in earthly form (see verse 13). The Lord tells Hagar that her child will be named *Ishmael* (*God hears*) because God has listened to her cries and cared for her in her affliction. Ishmael will become the ancestor to fierce bedouin tribes that live on the fringes of the wilderness (see also his genealogy in Genesis 25:12-18).

Hagar is amazed that she has seen God and lived to tell about it (compare Exodus 19:21; 33:20). In this episode, however, God sees and hears, and is seen and heard. Hagar is obedient to what she has seen and heard.

The Covenant of Circumcision (17:1-27)

When the child Ishmael is thirteen years old, Abraham and Sarah still have no offspring of their own. God comes to Abraham again, however, with a renewal of the promises of descendants and land (verses 1-8) and with the new covenant requirement of circumcision (verses 9-14).

Verses 1-8: God Almighty (*El Shaddai*) greets Abraham with commands and promises. To *walk before* God is to live one's life in a trusting, obedient relationship with God. To be *blameless* is to be found without fault in such a relationship. That God will *increase* (NIV) Abraham means not only that God will send him numerous descendants, but also that Abraham will abound in God's blessings. (See the comments on Genesis 15:7-21 concerning covenant.)

Abram (*exalted father*) will now be called Abraham (*father of a multitude*). Abraham's and Sarah's new names (see also verse 15) symbolize the important changes that their relationship to God will bring about. They are making a transition into a new life, and their names reflect this transition.

Abraham is promised descendants. He and his descendants are promised a homeland (*the land of Canaan*) and an abiding relationship with God (*I will be their God*).

Verses 9-14: God's covenant is not only with Abraham but also with the generations that will follow him. Because of this, each generation must wear the sign of this covenant. This sign (for Abraham's male descendants) is circumcision. Circumcision was also practiced by many other ancient peoples, such as the Egyptians and Edomites, perhaps for reasons of hygiene as well as for religious purposes.

For the people of Israel, however, circumcision is a sign in their very flesh that they are chosen by and committed to God. In later Scriptures, circumcision is spoken of not as a physical act, but as a symbol of being open and obedient to God (see, for example, Deuteronomy 30:6; also Colossians 2:11-13). This symbolic circumcision applies to all people, male and female.

Verses 15-21: *Sarai* is an older form of the name *Sarah*. Both mean *princess*. She is to become, according to God's promise, the mother of nations and kings.

Despite his previous encounters with God and his pledges of faith in God's promises, Abraham laughs at this promise (see also Genesis 18:10-12). His common sense tells him that this cannot be so. His patience with God has worn thin and he pleads for what he can see (the child Ishmael) rather than believing further in what he cannot see (the promised son). He asks that Ishmael may *live*, that is, thrive and prosper, with God's favor. Abraham is tired of waiting and wants to claim the promises now.

God is determined to have the last laugh, however. Despite Abraham's skepticism, the son will come, and the son's name will be Isaac (*he laughs*). Ishmael will be the father of *princes* (NRSV; NIV = *rulers*; compared with *kings* in verses 6, 16; see also the comments on Genesis 16:7-14). To Isaac, however, will belong the covenant heritage.

Promises and Punishment (18:1-33)

The Lord comes to Abraham in the form of three men, who eat a meal with him and bring him news both of birth (verses 1-15) and of judgment (verses 16-33).

Promises and Laughter (18:1-15)

Abraham may not know at first whom he is greeting but offers them the hospitality typically extended to strangers. He provides rest, shelter, food, and water in which to wash after their dusty travels. Abraham serves them meat (reserved for special occasions), bread (*cakes*), yogurt (*curds*), and milk.

The strangers' question in verse 9 is a clue that they are not ordinary visitors. They perhaps want to know where Sarah is so that she will be sure to hear what they say to Abraham about her. For the first time, the Lord gives Abraham a specific time when the promises of a son will be fulfilled. He and Sarah no longer have to wait in suspense. Now, however, Sarah cannot believe the time has really come. She thinks that her body is no longer capable of bearing a child, even a child promised by God.

Her laughter turns to fear, however, and she tries to protect herself by lying about what she did. The Lord's question in verse 14 strikes at the heart of the issue of faith: If God is God, why can't the promises be believed? At the time appointed by God, all doubts will be swept away in the reality of the promised son. Sarah's remaining doubts and fears cannot block God's intentions.

Intercession for Sodom and Gomorrah (18:16-33)

More of Abraham's responsibilities under the covenant are revealed in this episode. His relationship to God is not to be just one of obedient waiting and acceptance; it also involves active pursuit of righteousness and justice. Keeping the way of the Lord is more than circumcision and more than patience. He must live according to God's instructions and teach his descendants to do the same. Though God will overcome some human resistance (such as Sarah's and Abraham's laughter), the complete fulfillment of the covenant promises depends upon both God and Abraham (and his descendants).

By the time the men leave his camp, Abraham knows he is talking to the Lord God. God then gives Abraham a chance to do some reflection on how God's judgment and grace operate. The Lord tells Abraham where the "men" are going and for what purpose (verses 20-21). The Lord probably also tells Abraham why he is being told of this mission (verses 17-19). Once Abraham understands his responsibility to do righteousness and justice, he takes the opportunity to question God about its practice. He is to model his life according to the standards of righteousness and justice set by God, so he asks, how does God then do right (verse 25) and what does this mean for human beings?

Righteousness and justice are closely related to each other. Righteousness is being in right relationship to God, and includes awe, respect, trust, and obedience to God's laws. Justice is found in the practice of righteousness in daily life.

Abraham knows what God will find on the journey

and correctly assumes that it is not just knowledge but also justice that God seeks in Sodom and Gomorrah.

Understanding how justice and mercy (both divine and human) work is not always easy. In the Old Testament, the shedding of innocent blood is an offense to righteousness and justice (see, for example, Genesis 4:1-10; Deuteronomy 19:10). However, the innocent sometimes do suffer along with the guilty, especially in times of war (see, for example, Joshua 6:15-21; 7:16-26). In other cases, it is clearly stated that guilt and punishment are decided on an individual basis (see Ezekiel 14:12-14; 18:1-4, 25-32; also Genesis 6:1-8). In this case, Abraham pleads for the righteousness of a few to be grounds for sparing even the guilty.

In the end, the sins of Sodom and Gomorrah are so overwhelming that only the innocent are spared through God's mercy (see Genesis 19).

§ § § § § § §

The Message of Genesis 16–18

The stories in the book of Genesis tell us about people, such as Abraham, Sarah, Hagar, and Lot, and they tell us what these people are like. What do these stories reveal to us about what God is like?

§ God is the Redeemer who saves Hagar and Ishmael from death.

§ God is the Creator who overcomes both physical and spiritual barrenness and who brings life where there is no life.

§ God is the Partner who establishes a redeeming relationship with Abraham, with Ishmael, and (eventually) with Isaac.

§ God is the Judge who deals with human sin and who acts to establish divine justice and righteousness in the world.

§ God is the patient Teacher who leads and is revealed to the chosen people.

§ § § § § § §

PART NINE Genesis 19–20

Introduction to These Chapters

Chapter 19 deals with the fate of Sodom and Gomorrah and of Lot's family. Chapter 20 tells about how Abraham and Sarah try to fool Abimelech, the king of Gerar. These two chapters may be outlined as follows.

    I. Sodom and Gomorrah Destroyed (19:1-29)
   II. Lot's Descendants (19:30-38)
 III. Abraham, Sarah, and Abimelech (20:1-18)

Sodom and Gomorrah Destroyed (19:1-29)

Genesis 18:16-33 sets the stage for this story about what happens to Sodom and Gomorrah.

Verses 1-11: The *two angels* are two of the "men" who came to see Abraham (see Genesis 18). They are sent by God to investigate the conditions in Sodom and Gomorrah because an *outcry* has been raised against these cities (verse 13; see also 18:20). The King James Version translates *outcry* as *the cry of it,* that is, the sin itself cries out for God's attention (compare Genesis 4:8-10, where the blood of Abel cries to God from the ground). Sin thus makes itself known, especially the abundant sins of Sodom and Gomorrah.

This story presents the sins of the people of these cities as primarily sexual perversion (see verses 4-5). Later Scriptures also include references to injustice (see Isaiah 1:10-17; 3:8-12), adultery (see Jeremiah 23:14), and ignoring the poor and needy (see Ezekiel 16:49-50) among the sins of Sodom. God does not judge and punish on the outcry alone, however, but seeks firsthand knowledge of the situation.

Lot immediately offers the men hospitality as did Abraham, though the men are prepared to sleep in the streets. Lot insists that they come to his home, perhaps because he knows they will be accosted by the men of Sodom if they sleep outside. Once the men accept Lot's invitation, he is bound to offer them not only food and shelter but protection as well.

When the men of Sodom demand to know the visitors sexually (verse 5), Lot defends his visitors according to the standards of hospitality. He sacrifices his moral obligations to his daughters, however, by offering them to the mob in place of the visitors. Lot's offer is evidence of the abuse to which a father's control over his children could lead (or a husband's control over a concubine; see Judges 19:22-30). Later Israelite laws concerning the treatment of daughters and female slaves are perhaps in response to such abuse (see Exodus 21:7-11; Leviticus 19:20-22, 29).

The mob refuses Lot's pleas, saying that as an outsider (*alien*) he has no right to judge their behavior or to deny their demands. The angels rescue Lot and temporarily blind the men attacking the house (see also 2 Kings 6:18).

Verses 12-29: Even though Lot apparently believes what the two angels tell him about the coming destruction, he still hesitates to leave his home. It is only by God's mercy that he is forced to save his own life and the lives of his wife and daughters. Even then, he hesitates to flee to the hills, perhaps because he thinks they cannot travel fast enough to escape the destruction in the valley. The angels grant them safety in *Zoar* (meaning *small*).

The once-fertile valley is overwhelmed with burning brimstone (sulphur). Pits of sulphur and bitumen are found in this area even today (see also Genesis 14:10). Upheavals in the earth could have sent flaming rocks and liquid hydrocarbons raining down on the people and towns in the valley. The ruins of Sodom and Gomorrah may now lie under the southern end of the Dead Sea.

Lot's wife cannot resist a look back at what is happening to her former home despite the warnings of the angels (verse 17). She is perhaps overwhelmed by rock salt that is thrown up from the earth during the destruction.

Many large columns and pillars of salt can be seen today around the Dead Sea. The sea itself has a saltiness of 26 percent (compared to the 3.5 percent saltiness of the world's oceans). Fish cannot live in the sea because of the salt and because of the high magnesium content of the water. The salt comes from a mountain of rock salt that is at the southern end of the Dead Sea and from the high evaporation rate of the water. The surface of the sea is about 1,312 feet below sea level, and summer temperatures there average 104 degrees.

Abraham watches the destruction in silence, perhaps wondering what has happened to Lot and his family.

The writers of Genesis conclude their story of Sodom and Gomorrah with a comment on both God's saving actions and God's destructive actions (verse 29). Out of the destruction brought on by sin, God saves Lot because *God remembered Abraham* (see Genesis 18:22-33). To *remember* is not just to recall something. Remembering also involves action and commitment either on God's part (see, for example, Genesis 8:1; 9:15; Jeremiah 31:34) or on the part of human beings (see Micah 6:5; Deuteronomy 9:7). God remembers Abraham by showing mercy and grace, so that, after all, the righteousness of one may affect the fate of another.

Lot's Descendants (19:30-38)

Lot and his daughters move on into the hills, perhaps to escape the smoke and gases caused by the fires in the valley. They live in isolation, not knowing if they are the only people left alive on earth. The daughters were once betrothed (see verse 14), but now they are homeless and husbandless. The natural course of events in their lives has been disrupted and they fear that they will not be able to have children. They also fear that their family will become extinct.

Lot had tried to use them in a difficult situation (see verse 8); now they use him to get the children they desire. The name *Moab* means *of the same father*, and *Ben-ammi* means *son of paternal kin*. In years to come the Israelites do not always enjoy friendly relations with their Moabite and Ammonite cousins.

Abraham, Sarah, and Abimelech (20:1-18)

This story tells of a situation that is similar to the one described in Genesis 12:10-20. Abraham and Sarah travel to a different country where Abraham is afraid for his life because other men will desire his wife. In both cases, their attempts at deception lead to trouble for their hosts, and God must intervene to right the situation.

Verses 1-7: Abraham moves his flocks and family southwest of Canaan, finally stopping in Gerar. He presents Sarah as his sister (see verse 12) but fails to say she is also his wife. Marriage to a half-sister was allowed for a time (see also 2 Samuel 13:12) but was later forbidden (see Leviticus 18:9).

Sarah is now by her own admission *old* (see Genesis 18:11-12), perhaps around ninety-nine years old. Despite her age, however, she still commands the attention of Abimelech who takes her into his household to make her one of his wives or concubines. This puts in jeopardy God's intentions concerning the child promised to Abraham and Sarah. God then appears to Abimelech in a dream and reveals the truth to him (see also such dreams in Daniel 2; 4).

God acts to protect Abimelech in his innocence

because he acted in good faith. Once the king knows the truth, however, he must take responsibility for his actions. Taking Sarah as his wife would be a sin against God. He, Abraham, Sarah, and God's plans for the chosen people would suffer.

Verses 8-18: Abraham apparently does not consider the consequences of his actions for Sarah or for Abimelech. Abimelech has every right to rebuke him and to demand an explanation. Abraham then confesses his fear (verse 11) that is at the root of his deception. He is afraid there will be no *fear of God*, that is, no respect for moral or social obligations, in Gerar. In fact, Abraham is the one who shows no fear of God because fear also includes respect and honor for God's word. God's word to Abraham had been to trust that the great promises made to him would come true (see, for example, Genesis 12:1-3; 18:10). Abraham shows a distinct lack of trust.

Abimelech enriches Abraham and pays a large amount of money to ensure that Sarah's good reputation is restored. The king takes the responsibility for righting the wrong that Abraham began. Abraham then intercedes with God for Abimelech and his family (as in Genesis 18:22-33). As a *prophet* he is one who speaks for God to the people and with God on behalf of the people (see also, for example, Exodus 7:1-2; Numbers 21:7).

§ § § § § § §

The Message of Genesis 19–20

Over and over again, the stories in Genesis bear witness to certain truths about God's relationship to the world and to the chosen people. In chapters 19–20, we see that God acts to maintain justice and righteousness in the world and to safeguard the destiny of Abraham and Sarah. What else do these chapters reveal to us?

§ God has chosen the family of Abraham and Sarah with whom to have a special and redeeming relationship.

§ God guides and protects the covenant family.

§ God makes accommodation for human weakness, even within the covenant family.

§ God judges and punishes human sin.

§ God brings good out of evil for those who will listen to and obey God's voice.

§ § § § § § §

Genesis 21–23

Introduction to These Chapters

These chapters open with the birth of Isaac and close with the death of Sarah. In between these events lie episodes of conflict and of trial for Abraham and his family.

These three chapters may be outlined as follows.
 I. The Birth of Isaac (21:1-7)
 II. Hagar and Ishmael Are Banished (21:8-21)
 III. Abraham's Covenant with Abimelech (21:22-34)
 IV. God Tests Abraham (22:1-24)
 V. The Death of Sarah (23:1-20)

The Birth of Isaac (21:1-7)

God's benevolent presence comes to Sarah and brings the long-promised son. The name *Isaac* means *he laughs* (see also Genesis 17:16-19). When Isaac is eight days old, he is circumcised according to the covenant that Abraham made with God (see Genesis 17:9-14).

Sarah no longer laughs in disbelief at God's promises (see Genesis 18:9-15). Now she laughs in joy because of her child. Other people who hear of her good fortune will laugh in delight that God would bring this new life out of parents who are old (see 18:11). God answers the question of whether anything is too hard (wonderful) for the Lord with the reality of the promised child, Isaac.

Only God could say that Sarah would nurse her own child at ninety-nine years of age. No human being would make such an astonishing claim (verse 7) except one who hears and accepts the mysterious power of God to bring life where there is no life.

Hagar and Ishmael Are Banished (21:8-21)

God also brings life out of death for Hagar and Ishmael when they are driven from their home into the wilderness.

Verses 8-14: When Isaac is weaned at 2 or 3 years of age, Sarah demands that Abraham banish Hagar and Ishmael in order to protect Isaac's right of inheritance. It may be commonly assumed by their family and friends that Ishmael is Abraham's heir since he is the firstborn son.

God assures Abraham that both Isaac and Ishmael are included in God's plans for humankind. Through Isaac Abraham's line will continue and his descendants will identify themselves through Isaac's name (see, for example, Deuteronomy 1:8). God's great promises to Abraham (see Genesis 12:1-3) will be secured through Isaac, but Ishmael will not be abandoned. God will see to his future for Abraham's sake.

Hagar and Ishmael are sent off into the wilderness with only bread and a goatskin filled with water. Beersheba is in the northern Negeb at the junction of several trade routes. The town stands amid a series of chalk hills and is bordered on the southwest by a large area of sand dunes. Hagar and Ishmael are sent off into this arid and inhospitable region.

Verses 15-21: The name *Ishmael* means *God hears*, and God once again responds to the distress of Hagar and her child (see also Genesis 16:7-14). Ishmael is about fourteen years old. He is abandoned by his father and now even by his mother, who cannot stand to watch him die of thirst. God hears his cries, however, and enables Hagar to see the water that is available to save their lives. God tells Hagar to comfort Ishmael as well as to get him some water.

Their lives are not over by any means. God is *with* Ishmael, that is, God maintains a saving relationship with him so that Ishmael may fulfill the destiny set out for him by God.

Hagar takes over the responsibility that Abraham would have had for finding Ishmael a wife. He becomes the ancestor of the Bedouin tribes that live in the area of the wilderness of Paran between Canaan and Sinai. Many of his descendants still live in the rural areas of Saudi Arabia, though now they may drive pickup trucks instead of camels.

Abraham's Covenant with Abimelech (21:22-34)

Abraham and Abimelech formally conclude their differences and settle a dispute over water rights with a covenant.

Verses 22-24: Probably because of Abraham's initial dishonesty with him (see Genesis 20:1-18), Abimelech seeks a formal agreement with Abraham that will ensure honest dealings between the two of them from now on. Abimelech asks that Abraham be loyal (which includes friendship, kindness, and honesty) to him, to his family, and to the people of his land.

Abraham agrees, and they swear an oath of loyalty to each other with God as witness. Since God is called to be part of the oath, breaking the oath is considered to be breaking faith with God.

Verses 25-34: Abraham is a sojourner, an immigrant in the land of Abimelech. He and his family dig a well for their own use, but some of Abimelech's servants claim it for themselves. As a sojourner Abraham has the right to claim protection and sustenance under the authority of a king or chieftain in the land. He also must accept certain responsibilities for the privilege of living there. Thus, Abraham offers Abimelech sheep and oxen in exchange for official recognition of his claim to the well. The seven lambs are a gift given by Abraham in validation of their covenant.

Beersheba means *well of seven* or *well of the oath*.

The land to which Abimelech and Phicol return (verse 32) is not at that time known as the *land of the Philistines*. The Philistine people did not move into the coastal region of Canaan until around 1200 B.C. The writers of Genesis know the area of Gerar as belonging to the Philistines so that is how they identify it.

Abraham plants a tree at Beersheba and there worships God (see also Genesis 12:8). Beersheba continues to be an important religious sanctuary into the time of the prophet Amos (around 700 B.C.). Later generations of Israelites are told not to plant sacred trees in imitation of Canaanite cult practices (see Deuteronomy 16:21) in order to keep them from mixing the worship of God with the worship of idols.

God Tests Abraham (22:1-24)

This is a complex and unsettling story about the relationship between God and those who are called to be followers of God.

Abraham has lived through long years waiting for the promised son. Now he is told to give up his son and give up the promises of blessing that were to have come through Isaac. Not only is Abraham told to give up Isaac, but he must kill the boy himself and burn his body as an offering to God, the very God who made those great promises to him.

Verses 1-3: The exact location of the land *of Moriah* (verse 2) is unknown, but it has traditionally been associated with Jerusalem. The mount on which Abraham offers his sacrifice is believed to be where Solomon later built the first Temple and where the great mosque called the Dome of the Rock now stands.

Verses 4-8: Offering animal sacrifices as burnt offerings in worship of God has become an established practice. Thus, apparently no one suspects that anything is unusual about this sacrificial journey until Isaac questions his father about the animal (verse 7).

The storyteller does not tell us what is going on in Abraham's mind and heart at this point in the story. We see only Abraham calmly and deliberately obeying God's previous instructions. For his part, Isaac waits in silent trust except when he asks Abraham about the sacrificial animal.

Abraham's answer to Isaac's question (verse 8) is our only clue about what he is thinking and feeling about the situation. He knows that God will provide the sacrifice, but he does not know if Isaac, the gift of God, is the sacrifice that has already been provided.

Verses 9-14: Another summons comes from heaven that relieves Abraham of his awful task. He has passed the test and has proved that he truly fears God (verse 12). In this context, faith is spoken of as fearing God. Fear of the Lord is not just a feeling but is a combination of feelings, attitudes, and habits that govern a person's relationship to God. *Fear* includes reverence, trust, love, and an awesome respect and wonder at God's great and mysterious power. Fear and love of God always go together, for an absolute love of God demands undivided loyalty and total surrender of oneself to God. This is what Abraham has been willing to do.

Abraham gives Isaac up through his willingness to offer his son as a sacrifice to God. He receives him back through faith (see also Hebrews 11:17-19). Abraham knows that God will bring life out of death even though God's ways and purposes are not always clearly understood.

God provides a ram for the sacrifice in place of Isaac.

Because of this Abraham names that place *Adonai-yireh*, that is, *the LORD will provide* or *the LORD will see*. In the Old Testament it is not unusual for a place to be named after an encounter with God (see, for example, Genesis 16:13-14; 28:16-19).

Verses 15-19: God repeats the promises of Genesis 12:1-3 and 15:5 and swears an oath in the divine name (*By myself I have sworn*) that these promises will someday be fulfilled.

Verses 20-24: Abraham receives news of his brother's family (see also Genesis 11:27-29). This genealogy introduces Rebekah, who will become Isaac's wife (see Genesis 24).

The Death of Sarah (23:1-20)

When Sarah dies Abraham must seek a place to bury her, for they have been wanderers and have no property of their own.

Verses 1-2: Hebron is a town in the hills approximately nineteen miles south of Jerusalem.

Abraham goes into Sarah's tent to sit on the ground. There he wails, weeps, and expresses his grief over her death.

Verses 3-16: Abraham must now attend to the details of securing a grave for his wife. He is a resident alien in Canaan and must seek special authority to own land. The fact that he is well known and respected (*a mighty prince* or *the elect of God*) helps his cause.

He goes to the elders of the area who sit by the city gate and act as a governing council, and he asks them to intervene for him with the owner of the land he wants to buy. Despite his offer to *give* Abraham the property (verse 11), the owner apparently has no intention of giving it away. He finally asks a very high price for the land, and Abraham accepts it. The sale is witnessed and finalized. Abraham gets secure and permanent title to the land and its burial cave.

Verses 17-20: Sarah's body is carried to the cave on a litter and then laid on a shelf or niche that has been cut into the wall. Eventually, Abraham, Isaac, Rebekah, Leah, and Jacob will also be buried there (see Genesis 49:31). The site of this cave is now covered by a mosque which is one of the most sacred shrines in the Islamic faith.

§ § § § § § §

The Message of Genesis 21–23

In chapter 21 God answers the question posed in Genesis 18:14. Indeed, nothing is too hard for God who brings life where there is no life. The promised child has arrived. In chapter 23, Abraham buys property in the Promised Land and is no longer a landless sojourner. His possession of this relatively small plot of land both symbolizes and seals the promise that God made concerning the whole land of Canaan (see Genesis 12:5-7). In between these two great events is the story of how God tests Abraham. What does this story tell us about God, Abraham, and faith?

§ God calls, tests, and provides for the covenant family (see also 1 Corinthians 10:13).

§ Abraham hears, answers, and obeys.

§ Faith is a recognition and acceptance of the promise, the test, and the providential care of God (see also Hebrews 11:1).

Why does God test Abraham, and what does this mean for us?

§ Perhaps God tests Abraham because of his wavering and doubt in the past (see, for example, Genesis 17:17). The test will prove whether Abraham can still trust God even if he must give up Isaac, who is the tangible evidence of the truth of God's word as well as his beloved son.

§ This kind of test is perhaps one that must be faced by everyone who claims to follow God's word. Each of us is called to face this terrifying summons. Can we accept God as both the one who tests and the one who provides? Can we trust the promises in the face of seeming contradiction and disaster?

§ § § § § § §

Genesis 24–26

Introduction to These Chapters

In order for God's promises concerning Abraham's descendants to be fulfilled (see, for example, Genesis 13:16) Isaac must have a wife. As has been true in the past, God takes a hand in seeing that events work out as they should. This section also reports the death of Abraham, the birth of Jacob and Esau, and the blessing of Isaac.

Genesis 24–26 may be outlined as follows.
I. Isaac and Rebekah (24:1-67)
II. The Death of Abraham (25:1-18)
III. Birth and Rivalry of Jacob and Esau (25:19-34)
IV. The Blessings of Isaac (26:1-35)

Isaac and Rebekah (24:1-67)

Verses 1-9: Abraham gives the task of finding a wife for Isaac to his most trusted servant. The woman must not be a Canaanite but must be from among Abraham's kinsmen in his native Mesopotamia. This will ensure the legitimacy of the line through which God's covenant promises are fulfilled. The family of the bride must call on the name of the one true God (see verses 50-51). Neither must Isaac leave his home, because the fulfillment of the covenant is also tied to the Promised Land where he now lives.

In answer to his servant's doubts about the mission, Abraham repeats God's promises to him (verse 7; see also

Genesis 12:1-7) and declares his belief that God will aid the servant. God will be at work on behalf of the promises. The servant then swears an oath that he will fulfill Abraham's instructions under the penalty of a curse if he fails. He places his hand under Abraham's *thigh* (verse 9), that is, near his genitals, as a gesture that symbolizes his sincerity and seals the agreement. The thigh is related to vitality and procreation, which are believed to be gifts from God. To swear by the thigh is to swear by the power of life itself and to call God as a witness to the oath (see also Genesis 47:29).

Verses 10-33: The *city of Nahor* (NRSV; NIV = *town of Nahor*) in Mesopotamia is probably Haran (see Genesis 11:27-32). The servant opens his mission with a prayer. He asks for success in his task as evidence of God's steadfast love, or faithful loyalty, toward Abraham. He acknowledges that God has a particular woman in mind who is *chosen* (NIV; NRSV = *appointed*) to be Isaac's wife. He asks for a sign from God that he may know who she is.

Rebekah, who is the granddaughter of Abraham's brother, Nahor (see Genesis 22:20-23), greets the servant with the sign he asks for. She is also attractive and energetic. In response, the servant offers a short hymn of thanksgiving to God (verses 26-27).

Rebekah accepts the jewelry offered her by Abraham's servant, then runs to tell her family about him. A nose-ring, which is worn in the left nostril, is also a modern-day betrothal present among some peoples in Arabia.

Verses 34-51: In his statement to Rebekah's family the servant stresses the blessings from God that Abraham has enjoyed and the role of God in his mission to find a wife for Abraham's son. It is important for Rebekah and her family to understand that there is more at stake here than just finding a wife in Abraham's family in order to strengthen the family line. They must also know that God's larger purposes are at work here.

In response to the servant's request for an answer to his appeal (verse 49), Laban and Bethuel confess their belief that all these events come from God and so they can neither disapprove nor approve. They can only agree.

Verses 52-61: The negotiations sealing the marriage agreement are similar to practices known among other peoples of that day and region. The servant acts as the spokesman for Abraham, father of the groom, and Laban acts on behalf of the bride. It has been speculated that the reference to Bethuel in verse 50 is a later addition to the text. There is no reference to him in the exchange of gifts (verse 53) or in the negotiations about when Rebekah will leave (verse 55). This may mean that he is dead and that Rebekah's mother and brother are acting in his place (see also verse 28).

Rebekah's family is reluctant for her to leave, but she has no doubts about her decision and is ready to go. Her family sends her off with their blessings for fruitfulness and security in her new life (verse 60).

Verses 62-67: Isaac is perhaps meditating on his mother's death and on the bride who will be coming to him from so far away. Traditionally, the groom does not see the bride's face until after the wedding, so Rebekah veils her face when she and Isaac first meet.

The Death of Abraham (25:1-18)

As Abraham comes to the end of his life, his line is carried on and expanded through his many children. The relationship established between God and Abraham is continued as Isaac receives God's blessing and as Ishmael becomes the father of twelve tribes (see also Genesis 17:20).

Verses 1-6: Abraham's concubines are Hagar (see Genesis 16) and Keturah. The names of Keturah's descendants are both personal and tribal names. They become the ancestors of Arabian tribes living to the east of Canaan. These children receive *gifts* from Abraham, but it is Isaac who receives *all* (NRSV; NIV = *everything*), that is, the primary inheritance. This inheritance includes not only Abraham's considerable wealth in flocks and his land (see Genesis 23:17-20), but also the covenant promises (see Genesis 12:1-7; 17:21).

Verses 7-11: Abraham dies in *a good old age*, not only full of years but also full of contentment and satisfaction. He is buried in the cave that he bought when Sarah died (see Genesis 23) and is thus *gathered to his people.* Isaac and Ishmael together attend to his burial. Though destined for separate and distinct ways of life, they share the responsibility for seeing that their father is properly laid to rest.

Verses 12-18: Ishmael's descendants are both farmers (*their villages* [NRSV; NIV = settlements]) and nomads (*their encampments*). They live to the south and east of Canaan around the Arabian peninsula.

Birth and Rivalry of Jacob and Esau (25:19-34)

The family of Abraham is chosen by God and blessed by God, but it is also a family whose members are often in conflict with one another and with others.

Verses 19-23: Like Abraham and Sarah, Isaac and Rebekah face a time of barrenness and must wait for the power of God to grant them children (see also Genesis 18:9-14). Rebekah's joy soon turns to distress, however, as she realizes that all is not well with the children she carries. She goes, perhaps to a nearby sanctuary (see Genesis 21:33), to get an answer from God about how she can survive and what all this means.

God does not offer her comfort but tells her of the future. The children she is carrying are destined to be in conflict with each other. These children also represent nations that will extend this conflict. Though they are yet unborn, they are unequal. One is destined to serve, the other to be served (see also Genesis 27:40). Esau's descendants (the Edomites) will later be dominated by

Jacob's descendants (the Israelites), though the Edomites at times gain their independence (see for example, 1 Kings 11:14-25).

Verses 24-28: Esau's name is related to the Hebrew words for *hairy* and *red* (see also verse 30). Jacob's name is related to the Hebrew word for *heel*.

The boys grow into contrasting lifestyles; one is a hunter, the other a shepherd. The conflict between them is also reflected in their parents' favoritism.

The red lintel stew that Esau wants is thereafter related to his name and the name of his descendants, who were known as the Edomites. *Edom* is similar to the Hebrew word for *red*.

Though Esau has often been looked upon as dimwitted and as a glutton for trading his birthright for something to eat, it is possible that he is suffering from hypoglycemia (low blood sugar). If so, then he may certainly feel as though he is on the point of death. The symptoms of this illness include hunger and a craving for sweets, fatigue, confusion, and blackouts. The protein-rich lintel stew that he asks for is exactly what he needs to get his blood sugar back in balance.

Jacob apparently cares nothing for his brother's weakened condition but seeks to take advantage of it. He wants Esau's birthright, the double portion of inheritance that goes to the eldest son (see Deuteronomy 21:17). Later, Jacob will also trick Esau out of his blessing, the right to leadership of the family and to the covenant privileges (see also Genesis 27:35-36). The two men swear an oath in which Esau's inheritance is exchanged for Jacob's food.

The writers of this story interpret Esau's actions as despising or shunning his birthright. In fact, however, the story seems to indicate that he really has no choice when Jacob refuses to help him without payment (though see also Genesis 33 for a more friendly episode between the two men).

The Blessings of Isaac (26:1-35)

This chapter is a collection of stories about Isaac that focus on the blessings that come to him from God.

Verses 1-2: Isaac is forced to move from Beer-lahoi-roi (see Genesis 25:11) to Gerar because of famine. Abraham had once been forced to move to Egypt because of famine (see Genesis 12:10-20), but God tells Isaac not to go to Egypt. He and his family are to stay in the land that God will one day give to his descendants. This area between Egypt and Canaan became part of the nation of Israel during the reigns of King David (1000-961 B.C.) and King Solomon (961-922 B.C.).

Abimelech is king of the people living in this area, but these people were not called Philistines in Isaac's day. The Philistine people settled along the coast of Palestine around 1200 B.C., so the writers of Genesis know the area of Gerar as belonging to the Philistines and identify it that way (see also Genesis 21:34).

Verses 3-5: God's promises to Isaac reaffirm the promises made to Abraham in years past: possession of the land (see Genesis 12:7), many descendants (see Genesis 15:5), and being a source of blessing for the nations (see Genesis 12:1-3). God is faithful to these promises because Abraham was obedient to God (see Genesis 18:19; 22:15-18). Isaac's inheritance includes the covenant promises (see Genesis 17:19-21).

Verses 6-11: Isaac trusts God to provide food for his family in Gerar, but he does not trust God to protect him from men who might desire his wife. Abraham also showed this lack of trust, which made trouble for him and for others (see also the comments on Genesis 12:10-20; 20:1-7). Isaac's attempted deception could have ended disastrously for Rebekah and for the community in which they are guests. As in the two previous episodes involving Abraham and Sarah, the community would have suffered the consequences for breaking the law against adultery.

Verses 12-16: As his father did before him, Isaac manages to get out of his deception with no permanent harm done. Indeed, he prospers greatly as a visitor in Gerar. The blessings God promises him (verses 3-4) are not just for the future but are also for now. Material abundance is his to enjoy. His crops produce well, his flocks and herds multiply, and he has a great household with many family members and servants. All this comes because of God's blessing, for the people of Gerar try to deny him water (see also Genesis 21:25-31) and they eventually ask him to move on because he is becoming *too powerful* for them.

Verses 17-22: Water is a precious and vital resource in this arid land, and disputes over water continue. The two disputed wells are called *Esek*, meaning *contention*, and *Sitnah*, meaning *enmity*. Finally, at the place he calls *Rehoboth*, meaning *broad places* or *room*, Isaac and his household find the space they need. Space and water are important resources for people still without a land to call their own.

Verses 23-33: These verses may be divided into two sections, verses 23-25 and verses 26-33. Each section contains a recognition and affirmation of Isaac's blessed position in the world.

In the first section, it is God who comes to Isaac with further assurances (*do not be afraid*) that God's blessings and presence will continue to be his (for Abraham's sake; see also Genesis 19:29). Isaac responds by building an altar and worshiping God (*called on the name of the LORD*; see also Genesis 12:7-8). He also responds by settling in this Promised Land. He stakes his claim, so to speak, as he pitches his tents and digs another well. He claims the promises of blessing and prosperity by establishing his access to water, which is a necessary resource for people, animals, and crops to flourish in this dry land.

In the second section, earthly powers affirm and recognize Isaac's blessed status. Abimelech seeks a covenant with Isaac that will officially establish good relations between them. They will live in *peace*. Peace not only means an absence of warfare but also includes everything that is necessary for a full, satisfying life (health, material comforts, and security).

Again Isaac finds water. He has moved from famine (verse 1) to abundance, which is summed up in the presence of life-giving water. *Shibah* means *oath* (see also Genesis 21:30-31 on the naming of Beersheba).

Verses 34-35: Unlike Abraham and Isaac, Esau marries women who are outside the covenant family. These wives are a source of bitter disappointment and sorrow for Isaac and Rebekah. Through these marriages, Esau takes another step away from the covenant family that will become Israel and another step toward the destiny laid out for him before his birth (see Genesis 25:21-23).

§ § § § § § §

The Message of Genesis 24–26

God continues to act to protect the destiny of the covenant family. Even so, the members of this special family are human beings who, at times, fail God and one another. In these chapters we are told about the end of Abraham's life and about the continuation of the covenant family into the second and third generations. What do these stories show us about the relationships within this very special family?

§ Abraham's life has not been one of unbroken faith. He has his moments of doubt and weakness. Through the years, however, his faith proves to be stronger than his doubt.

§ Abraham, Isaac, Rebekah, Esau, and Jacob do not always live within God's will.

§ Though God's blessings and promises bring material prosperity for Abraham (see also Genesis 24) and Isaac, these circumstances do not guarantee them a happy family life. Strife and misunderstanding are evident even in the chosen family.

§ The family somehow holds together and moves on into the future with God's help and guidance.

§ § § § § § §

PART TWELVE Genesis 27–29

Introduction to These Chapters

This portion of the Genesis narrative continues the stories about Isaac, Jacob, and Esau.

These chapters may be outlined as follows.
   I. Jacob Receives Isaac's Blessing (27:1-40)
  II. Jacob Must Flee (27:41-46)
 III. Jacob's Dream at Bethel (28:1-22)
 IV. Jacob Marries Leah and Rachel (29:1-35)

Jacob Receives Isaac's Blessing (27:1-40)

Jacob and Rebekah trick Isaac into giving Jacob the blessing that Isaac intends for Esau.

Verses 1-4: Isaac wants to formally transfer the blessings of prosperity and security (see verses 27-29) that he has enjoyed to his beloved son Esau (see Genesis 25:28). It is customary for such a blessing to pass from the father to the eldest son, but a father may instead choose a younger son to receive it. In this case, God intends that the younger son will eventually be the stronger (see Genesis 25:23).

Isaac's words carry special weight because they are like his "last will and testament." Deathbed blessings are especially important (see also, for example, Genesis 48:10-20; Deuteronomy 33). Isaac, however, will live approximately another sixty years (see Genesis 35:28-29).

Verses 5-29: Rebekah does not trust God to see that Jacob is truly blessed and is given his proper place in the covenant family and in history. She knows the power of the blessing that Isaac is about to deliver, so she takes matters into her own hands to see that Jacob is the recipient. Jacob does not hesitate to lie to his father or to take advantage of his father's blindness.

Isaac's blessing (verses 28-29) grants Jacob fertility of the land, prosperity, and power over his own family and his neighbors. Thus God's intentions for Jacob and Esau (see Genesis 25:23) are reinforced even though Isaac does not know that he is doing it. There is more at stake here than just the fate of the two brothers. They will become nations for whom God has particular plans.

To be blessed is to have good health, long life, material prosperity, and many descendants, and to have the security in which to enjoy these benefits. To be cursed is to endure illness, childlessness, famine, domination by other peoples, or even death.

Verses 30-40: Isaac and Esau are heartsick over what has happened, but nothing can be done to change it. Once spoken, the power of the blessing has been released and it cannot be recalled. This has to do with the belief that the spoken word has a life of its own and has the power in and of itself to cause things to happen in the natural world. This belief is grounded in the power of God's words that brought the world into being (see Genesis 1) and may also be seen in the power granted to the words of prophets whom God has called to speak (see, for example, Jeremiah 1:9-10). Thus, Jacob must remain blessed.

The name *Jacob* means *he takes by the heel* or *he supplants.* Jacob schemes to get Esau's birthright (see the comments on Genesis 25:27-34) and now tricks him out of his father's blessing.

The *one blessing* (verse 38) that Isaac may now give Esau is a mixed one. Esau will not enjoy the fertility and material prosperity that Jacob will have because Esau must live in a less fertile and less well-watered land. He will survive, however, and though his people are destined to serve Jacob's people, they will eventually gain their independence.

Esau will become the father of the Edomite nation. Edom is east of southern Canaan in what is now Jordan. Edom was under Israelite control during the reign of King David (1000–961 B.C.), but successfully revolted during the reign of King Solomon (961–922 B.C.).

Jacob Must Flee (27:41-46)

Jacob and Rebekah pay a price for their deceit. Jacob must flee from Esau's vengeance, and Rebekah must give up her favorite son. Though she believes that Jacob must be gone only *a while*, he will not return for twenty years. (The Scripture does not say whether Rebekah is still alive when he returns.) She is afraid that Esau will kill Jacob and that Esau will be slain as a murderer. Though she favors her younger son, she does not want to lose either of her children and the promises for the future that they hold.

Rebekah's brother Laban lives in Haran, a city in Mesopotamia to which Abraham's family had migrated before Abraham moved on to Canaan (see also Genesis 11:27-32; 24:1-67). Jacob will be safe there from Esau's wrath and may also find there a wife who will be part of the covenant family. Esau had married women of Canaan who had no allegiance to the God of Abraham and Isaac (see the comments on Genesis 26:34-35). If Jacob is to bear the blessings and promises passed down from his father and grandfather, he must have a wife who will reinforce the special relationship that his family has with God.

Jacob's Dream at Bethel (28:1-22)

Jacob becomes an exile from his immediate family, but God is with him. God establishes a relationship with Jacob in which the promises made to Abraham and Isaac will be kept alive.

90

Verses 1-5: Paddan-aram is the region in northern Mesopotamia that includes the city of Haran. *Bethuel* is Abraham's nephew (see also Genesis 22:20-23; 25:20) and is an *Aramean,* one of the descendants of Shem (see Genesis 10:22-23). The Aramean people lived in tribal groups throughout northern Mesopotamia and Syria. (On the significance of Isaac's instructions to Jacob concerning his future wife, see the comments on Genesis 27:41-46.)

Isaac offers a benediction over Jacob as he leaves. He asks that God pass the blessings given to Abraham on to Jacob (compare Genesis 12:1-7; 15:18-19). The *land where you now live as an alien* is the land of Canaan. Though Abraham and Isaac both were promised the possession of this land for their descendants and both prospered in this land, their family is still a guest here. Jacob must wander still and sojourn in another land before he comes back to the Promised Land.

Verses 6-9: Esau perhaps thinks that his marriages to pagan women have somehow caused him to lose out on his father's blessing. He takes a wife who is the daughter of Ishmael, Abraham's son by his concubine, Hagar (see Genesis 16:1-15; 21:8-21), in an effort to please his mother and father (see also Genesis 26:34-35). He, too, maintains some part of the special relationship that God has chosen to have with the family of Abraham.

Verses 10-17: Jacob travels northward into the hill country that will later become part of the Northern Kingdom of Israel.

In his dream, Jacob sees a ladder or stairway that links heaven and earth. God's angels or messengers are traveling between heaven and earth, but it is the Lord God who speaks to Jacob while standing *above* or *beside* him. God tells Jacob that the great promises made to Abraham and Isaac are now passed on to him (verses 13-14). The covenant relationship is now confirmed with this new generation of the covenant family (compare Genesis 12:1-7; 15:5; 17:7-8; 22:16-18; 26:24-25).

God also promises Jacob that the two of them will have a very personal relationship. God will be with Jacob, will keep him safe, and will bring him back to this Promised Land (verse 15).

When he awakens, Jacob realizes that, even though he is far from his family and home, he is not far from the God of his fathers. God dwells here, too, and opens contact between heaven and earth.

Verses 18-22: Jacob responds to this revelation by consecrating this place to the worship of God. The name *Bethel* means *house of God.* On his return to Canaan twenty years later, he sets up an altar here (see Genesis 35:6-7). Bethel became an important sanctuary during the time of the judges and was one of the leading centers for worship in the Northern Kingdom of Israel from the time of King Jeroboam I (922-901 B.C.) to the reign of King Josiah (640-609 B.C.). The stone is a "spiritual milestone."

Jacob also responds to God's revelation with a vow. Note, however, that Jacob uses the word *if.* His promises to God are conditional, but God's promises to him are not. He will look to God's presence to go with him for protection, for sustenance, and for guidance. Jacob will accept the Lord as his God if God fulfills the promises made to him. Then, he will maintain the sanctuary he has set up and will support it with his tithe.

Jacob Marries Leah and Rachel (29:1-35)

God guides Jacob's journey to bring him and his mother's family together.

Verses 1-12: The land of the people of the east is Mesopotamia. These easterners are Arameans (see Genesis 28:2). The well in Haran is probably to be shared equally by several families, so the stone covering the well is large enough that it takes more than one person to move it. Jacob is so inspired by Rachel's appearance, however, that he summons the strength to move the stone by himself. Jacob's kiss of greeting is apparently acceptable, for women at this time and place have more freedom concerning their public behavior than they do in Near Eastern society later on.

Verses 13-30: Laban warmly greets Jacob as his kinsman but is not above taking advantage of his young homeless nephew. Even though he is a guest, Jacob may continue to help with the sheep and to fulfill other duties in Laban's household. Laban then strikes a bargain with Jacob that assures a husband for his daughters and also assures him of Jacob's labors for fourteen years.

Leah's eyes are *weak* (NIV; NRSV = *lovely*) or lacking in luster. Jacob agrees to serve Laban for seven years because he cannot afford the gifts that are customarily given to the bride's family (see Genesis 24:50-53).

The bride wears a veil at the wedding ceremonies and also, apparently, through the wedding night. Jacob, whose deception at home brought him to this place (see Genesis 27:1-45), is now the one who is deceived. He must wait a week for the completion of Leah's wedding festivities; then he may marry Rachel. The price for Rachel is also seven years of service.

Verses 31-35: According to Old Testament belief, God controls the conception of life. Having children is evidence of God's favor and blessing (see, for example, Genesis 4:1; 25:21). Being barren is a great tragedy and, in some cases, is believed to come from God (see, for example, Genesis 20:18; 30:2). God takes pity on Leah because she is unloved. The names she gives these sons reflect the fact that Leah believes they are born because of God's mercy. *Reuben* means *See, a son. Simeon* is similar to the Hebrew word for *heard. Levi* is similar to the word for *joined. Judah* is similar to the word for *praise.*

§ § § § § § §

The Message of Genesis 27–29

These chapters reveal that the members of the covenant family are still often in conflict with one another, even in this third generation. Jacob especially is a man of conflict. At one time or another he is at odds with Esau, Isaac, Laban, Leah, and also eventually with Rachel (see Genesis 30:1-2). Yet these stories leave no doubt that Jacob is also a man in a special relationship with God.

§ Jacob and Rebekah lie and cheat to get what they want from Isaac. They take matters into their own hands to see that the promises of Genesis 25:23 are fulfilled. Even later prophets use Jacob's behavior as a negative example in their preaching (see Hosea 12:2-4).

§ Jacob becomes a fugitive who is outside the protection and comfort of his family and who is without anyone to offer him hospitality. It is when he is most isolated and vulnerable that God comes to meet him (Genesis 28:10-17).

§ We do not know why God chooses Jacob to inherit the promises given to Abraham and Isaac. We only know that Jacob is to play an important role in God's plans for humankind and that Jacob's life is in God's care.

§ Jacob is the blessed one. Like his father and grandfather before him, however, he must wait for the fulfillment of God's word to him.

§ God does grant Jacob success, though why he has been chosen remains a mystery. The family of Jacob becomes the people of Israel who are a source of blessing for all the families of the earth (see also Genesis 12:1-3).

§ The story of Jacob's life (which continues through Genesis 50) shows that God's purposes in the world will be fulfilled, though we do not know how or why.

§ § § § § § §

Genesis 30–32

Introduction to These Chapters

Jacob has eleven children and prosperous flocks before God finally calls him to return to Canaan. These events are described in chapters 30–32, which may be outlined as follows.

I. Jacob Prospers (30:1-43)
    A. God sends Leah and Rachel children (30:1-24)
    B. Jacob grows rich (30:25-43)
II. Jacob Leaves for Canaan (31:1-55)
III. Jacob Wrestles with "a Man" (32:1-32)

Jacob Prospers (30:1-43)

Jacob must go through continued conflict with his wives and his father-in-law, but his family and his riches grow.

God Sends Leah and Rachel Children (30:1-24)

Verses 1-13: Like Sarah (see Genesis 11:30) and Rebekah (see Genesis 25:21), Rachel suffers a time of barrenness. She and Leah are still rivals for Jacob's affection and for the fulfillment and power that come through having children. (See also the comments on Genesis 29:31.)

Rachel may legally seek a child of her own by having her maid bear a child by Jacob (see also the comments on Genesis 16:1-6). God judges Rachel, that is, grants her justice, by giving her a son through Bilhah. The name *Dan* is related to the Hebrew for *judged* or *vindicated*. The name *Naphtali* is related to the Hebrew word for *contest*.

Rachel's success prompts Leah to also seek children through her maid. Zilpah gives birth to Gad (*fortune* or *luck*) and Asher (*happy*).

Verses 14-24: The mandrake plant (sometimes called the May apple or Devil's apple) grows in Egypt and Palestine. Its juice and gum contain a strong narcotic that was used to bring on sleep, kill pain, increase ardor, and overcome barrenness. Thus, the rival sisters strike a bargain over access to Jacob and to the "medicine" that they believe can cure their barrenness.

The bargain works for both of them. Leah names her fifth and sixth sons Issachar (*hire* or *reward*) and Zebulun (*honor*). Her daughter is named Dinah (*judgment*).

The mandrake potion would help to quiet Rachel's anxieties and bring on a more relaxed and tranquil state of mind. Whether or not she uses this medicine, however, Rachel's new fertility is clearly credited to God by the writers of this story. Throughout the book of Genesis, it is God and only God who may bring life where there is no life. God does not just mentally remember Rachel, but acts on her behalf (see also Genesis 19:29; 21:1-2). Joseph (meaning *he adds*) is a gift of God's grace to Rachel and Jacob.

Jacob Grows Rich (30:25-43)

Jacob has now served the required seven years as his gift to Laban for the right to marry Rachel. He is ready to return to his homeland, but Laban does not want to let him go.

Verses 25-36: Laban has learned by an omen that his prosperity comes from Jacob's skill with cattle and from God's blessings through Jacob. He makes another bargain with Jacob but again seeks to manipulate the deal to his advantage (compare Genesis 29:21-30).

Since animals with such markings are uncommon, Laban feels he is safe in agreeing to let Jacob have any dark-colored sheep and multicolored goats from his flocks. Even so, he has his sons take all such animals out of his flocks.

Verses 37-43: Jacob, however, has his own plans for outwitting Laban. He takes the branches of trees and peels the bark so that they have light and dark stripes. In ancient times, breeders believed that the breeding female animal could be influenced by what she sees to produce a certain color offspring. Thus, seeing the striped sticks would cause the goats to conceive striped or multicolored kids. The female sheep are exposed to the striped and dark-colored goats and thus conceive dark or multicolored lambs.

As his father and grandfather before him (see Genesis 26:12; 13:1-2), Jacob prospers even though he is a sojourner without all the advantages of living in his own land. God is indeed with Jacob (see Genesis 28:15). Though they may resort to the folk ways of mandrakes and striped rods to bring the blessings of fertility, Jacob and his family are under the greater power and care of the Lord God, who watches over these chosen ones (see also Genesis 31:6-10).

Jacob Leaves for Canaan (31:1-55)

This is a story of departure, confrontation, and resolution. In the midst of the very human feelings and struggles of the story, however, God's influence is plainly seen.

Verses 1-16: Jacob had intended to leave Haran for Canaan six years earlier (see Genesis 30:25-26), but the time was not right. Now, relations with Laban and his family have become hostile, and God calls Jacob to leave for home.

Jacob's declaration to Rachel and Leah (verses 5-13) is at the heart of the whole story of Jacob's sojourn in

Haran (Genesis 29–31). Laban cheats, and Jacob resorts to his own cunning and to folk magic, but God has the controlling hand in this situation (compare Joseph's statement to his brothers in Genesis 50:20). God's purposes are at work beyond and behind the rivalries and necessities of daily life. The God who appeared to Jacob at Bethel (see Genesis 28:10-22) is at work in this foreign land, and God's promises to Jacob are being kept.

Rachel and Leah readily agree to leave their father's household. In their view, he has cheated them out of their rightful share of the wealth he has gained from Jacob's labor. At this time, a woman may keep part of the bridal payment for herself according to the laws of Hurrian society (which some scholars believe is related to the society of the patriarchs). Rachel and Leah feel that their father has treated them as foreign women who do not have all the rights normally given to native women in their society.

Verses 17-24: The word translated *household gods* in verses 19 and 34 is *teraphim*, which means *idols*. Laban refers to them as gods (verse 30), as does Jacob when he quotes Laban (verse 32). These are figurines that are sometimes shaped like human beings and used for divination (see, for example, Ezekiel 21:21) or as cult objects (see Judges 17:1-6). In this case, the possession of such idols may represent a claim to family leadership and property.

Verses 25-35: Laban still considers his daughters to be part of his household, probably because Jacob had more or less indentured himself to Laban. He complains again of being cheated and of being denied the customary rituals of farewell (see also Genesis 24:55-61). The key problem for Laban, however, is the loss of his household gods.

Rachel has already decided that her father is not going to deal honestly with Jacob or with her and Leah (see verses 14-16), so she acts to take the law into her own hands and protect her position. Formal transfer of the idols to Jacob would have validated Jacob's claim to his flocks and would have been proof that Laban had released him and his wives.

As important as these idols are to Laban, Rachel ridicules them to some extent by sitting on them. As important as they may be legally, they deserve no real respect. Rachel proves herself to be as cunning as her father and her husband, for Laban does not find his idols. In the end, he carries on as if he is indeed still in control of Jacob's property but has decided to be generous (see verse 43).

Verses 36-42: Jacob defends himself and declares his honesty and faithfulness in his service to Laban. It is not to himself that he gives the credit, however. He knows that all his good fortune is from God. Jacob knows God as the God of his father and grandfather (see Genesis 28:13), whose presence is active in his life. The title *Fear of Isaac* (verse 42) may also mean the *Awesome One of Isaac* or the *kinsman of Isaac* (see also Genesis 26:24).

Verses 43-55: Jacob and Laban make a covenant of friendship between them. They agree that Jacob will care for Leah and Rachel and treat them well. They also establish a boundary between their territories, which will eventually become Israel and Syria. The Aramaic name of the boundary marker is *Jegar-sahadutha* and the Hebrew name is *Galeed* (also called *Gilead*). Both of these names mean *the heap of witness*. Neither man will cross the boundary with hostile intentions.

This place is also called *Mizpah* (*watchpost*) because Laban and Jacob call on God to witness their covenant and to monitor their faithfulness to the covenant. Since God is asked to participate in the agreement, breaking the agreement becomes an offense against God as well as against the covenant partner. Verse 49 is known as the "Mizpah Benediction."

Abraham is Jacob's grandfather. Nahor is Abraham's

brother and Laban's grandfather. Terah is the father of Abraham and Nahor (see Genesis 11:27; 22:20-23).

The covenant ceremony is completed with a sacrificial offering (see also Genesis 15) and with a covenant meal.

Jacob Wrestles with "a Man" (32:1-32)

God is with Jacob on his homeward journey. Though Jacob anticipates a meeting with his brother, Esau, he will meet God first in a life-changing encounter.

Verses 1-2: The hosts of God are again revealed to Jacob, and he sees the connections that exist between heaven and earth, between his path and God's path (see also Genesis 28:12-17). The name *Mahanaim* is related to the Hebrew for *two camps.*

Verses 3-8: Esau has settled in Edom, east of Canaan (see the comments on Genesis 25:23; 27:39-40). Jacob, though not confessing his wrongdoing toward his brother, wants Esau to know that he is not coming back deceitfully but openly and with good intentions. Esau's response is ambiguous, and Jacob prepares for the worst.

Verses 9-12: In his fear, Jacob turns to God in prayer. He confesses his unworthiness for the lovingkindness and faithfulness that God has shown him in his abundant material blessings and large family. Nevertheless, he is able to base his plea for help on God's call to return to Canaan (see Genesis 31:3) and on God's promises concerning his descendants (see also Genesis 28:13-14).

Verses 13-32: Jacob goes on to take other precautions against Esau's possible wrath. He hopes to appease Esau with gifts and thus atone for the past.

God came to Jacob when he was alone on his journey to Haran (see Genesis 28:10-22). Now God comes to Jacob again when he spends the night alone before facing Esau. The exact identity of the *man* with whom Jacob wrestles is not explained. At the end of the experience Jacob believes that he has seen God *face to face* (verse 30), so this man may be some manifestation or representative of God.

The wrestling match is a draw until the man touches Jacob's hip socket and injures him, but Jacob still will not let him go. Jacob demands and receives a blessing. This blessing comes in the form of a name change. Instead of being called *Jacob* (*he supplants*; see Genesis 25:23-26) he is now called *Israel* (*God strives* or *striver with God*). A name change is symbolic of a new identity and a new way of life (see also Genesis 17:5). Jacob has striven both with God and with human beings (particularly with Esau and Laban). He has proved himself an able and willing striver who no longer will need to resort to deceit or seek to supplant anyone. (Knowing someone's name also grants some control over that person, so the man will not tell Jacob his own name.)

Jacob calls this place *Peniel* (Penuel), which means *the face of God*. Many place names in the book of Genesis come from someone's encounter with God (see, for example, Genesis 16:13-14; 22:14).

In honor of Jacob's injury, the Israelites are said to not eat the sciatic muscle in an animal, though there is no other mention of this dietary rule in the Bible.

§ § § § § § §

The Message of Genesis 30–32

Jacob serves his time as an exile from his homeland. He eventually leaves for home with a new relationship to God, with wives and children born into the covenant family, and with material riches. Even so, none of this was accomplished easily because he and his family faced barrenness, family conflicts, and legal questions that had to be resolved. It is Jacob's relationship with God, however, which gives meaning to all these struggles. What can we say about this relationship?

§ God knows Jacob and has plans for him even before his birth (see Genesis 25:23-26).

§ God calls and Jacob responds, though not always with the utmost faith (see Genesis 28:10-22; 32:1-8).

§ God's name reveals something about what God is like, and God is known to Jacob as the *God of Abraham* and the *Fear of Isaac*. God is not distant but establishes a close relationship with Jacob's family. Thus, Jacob knows God in a personal way. He even has a new name, *Israel* (*he who strives with God*), which symbolizes this kinship.

§ Jacob gives his name to his descendants, the *people of Israel*. They, too, know God in a very personal way. They, too, struggle with God and are blessed by God.

§ Jacob comes out of his encounter with God with a new name but also with a limp. He is blessed but also weaker. From the story of Jacob's life and the history of the people of Israel, we may see that having a personal relationship with God does not necessarily lead to a life free of conflict. Instead we see that the relationship itself may bring new responsibilities, risks, and costs. New Testament teachings about discipleship reflect this same theme of blessing/cost (see, for example, Mark 8:34-35; 10:35-45).

§ § § § § § §

GENESIS

Genesis 33–36

Introduction to These Chapters

These chapters close the second large section of material in the book of Genesis that began in Genesis 12 with the call of Abraham. The story of the patriarchs Abraham, Isaac, and Jacob is followed by the story of Joseph (Genesis 37–50).

These chapters may be outlined as follows.
  I. Jacob and Esau Are Reconciled (33:1-20)
 II. Shechem and Dinah (34:1-31)
III. Jacob Comes to Mamre (35:1-29)
IV. The Descendants of Esau (36:1-43)

Jacob and Esau Are Reconciled (33:1-20)

Verses 1-17: Despite Jacob's fears (see Genesis 32:6-8), he and Esau meet in peace. Jacob humbles himself before his brother by bowing seven times before they embrace. His gifts to Esau (see Genesis 32:13-20) are evidence of his goodwill, of his gratitude for Esau's welcome, and of God's blessings to him. Thus, Jacob faces God and his brother before coming home, and he finds strife and favor with both. In Esau's acceptance he sees the same acceptance he is granted from God (33:10).

Jacob has not abandoned his old deceptive ways entirely, for he does not openly decline Esau's invitation to stay in *Seir* (that is, Edom, Esau's homeland). Jacob intends to go on to Canaan but, for reasons that are not clear, does not tell Esau this. He is perhaps still skeptical about Esau's goodwill toward him, and he may also be impatient to come once again into the land that God has promised him.

Succoth (*booths*) is near Peniel (see Genesis 32:30), east of the Jordan River approximately halfway between the Sea of Galilee and the Dead Sea. Booths are rough, temporary shelters constructed of brush or tree branches. They are used as shelters for livestock or field workers and for soldiers on battlefields.

Verses 18-20: The city of Shechem is west of the Jordan River in what later are known as the Samaria Hills. The town is at the intersection of important north-south and east-west travel routes. Paddan-aram is the area around Haran in northern Mesopotamia (see also Genesis 28:1-2). The *sons of Hamor* are the Canaanite leaders of the town. *Shechem* is also a person (verse 19; chapter 34) who is a member of this clan. It is significant that Jacob settles in Shechem on his return to Canaan, because this is where God first promised Abraham possession of this land for his descendants (see Genesis 12:1-7).

Jacob is granted the right to own property here even though he is legally still a sojourner in the land (see also the comments on Genesis 23:1-20). Jacob's son, Joseph, is later buried on this property (see Joshua 24:32). In buying this property, Jacob has made a symbolic claim to the whole land which is his according to God's promise. He makes a further claim to the land on God's behalf by setting up an altar to God and by naming this place *El-Elohe-Israel* (*God, the God of Israel*).

Jacob and his family live in Shechem for eight to ten years, though they do not always enjoy friendly relations with their Canaanite neighbors (see Genesis 34). The well that Jacob digs here is where Jesus talks with the woman of Samaria (see John 4).

Shechem and Dinah (34:1-31)

Jacob's children have now grown into adulthood. This next generation of the covenant family is beginning to assert itself; in this case, with violent results. This story tells about individual Israelites and Canaanites who fail to learn to live together in honor and peace. Through these individuals, the story may also reflect the difficulties that the peoples, clans, and societies in Canaan had in sharing the land with one another.

Verses 1-7: Dinah is raped by Shechem, the son of a leading citizen. Jacob reacts cautiously, and his sons take it upon themselves to deal with what has happened. That he *had done a disgraceful thing* (NIV; NRSV = *committed an outrage*) *in Israel* means that Shechem's crime has affected the whole covenant community. In the Old Testament there is a strong sense of community solidarity in which the actions or fate of an individual affect everyone in the community. *Israel* here does not mean just Jacob (see Genesis 32:28), but includes all of the Israelite community.

Verses 8-24: Hamor makes no mention of the wrong done to Dinah, but seeks to settle the controversy with an arrangement that he believes will be an advantage to both families. He sees economic and political advantages for himself and his neighbors by making peace with the prosperous Israelites and by gaining access to their daughters in marriage.

Circumcision is required for any male who is to be part of the covenant community (see Genesis 17:9-14). To the Canaanites it would have no such religious significance, but would only be a means to gain acceptance by the Israelites.

Verses 25-31: Jacob has allowed Dinah to stay in Shechem's house, perhaps in the belief that the agreement with his family and neighbors will be honored on both sides. Simeon and Levi, however, strike at the Canaanites while they are recovering from their surgery. Other sons of Jacob then loot the city and take both goods and captives for themselves.

Jacob rebukes his sons for their vengeance. They have

violated his good faith as well as that of the Canaanites. They have also put all of their family in danger of retaliation from other natives of the land. Their actions have only made a bad situation worse. The sons ignore Jacob's arguments, however, and seek only to justify their actions. The story ends on this note of disagreement and leaves unresolved the debate between Jacob and his sons.

Jacob's judgment on his sons is found in Genesis 49:5-7. He declares that their violence is unjustified and dangerous to the community of faith. They are therefore scattered. (A later law in Deuteronomy 22 deals with such a situation between Israelites.)

Jacob Comes to Mamre (35:1-29)

This chapter shows especially how the book of Genesis draws on different sources or strains of historical materials and traditions (see also the Introduction on pages 7-10). Though the events told here are in roughly chronological order, they are mixed with information about death and crime within the covenant family and with genealogical information. Chapter 35 is a "patchwork" of stories and historical notes that finally bring Jacob home to his father.

Verses 1-4: In the rape of Dinah, the community of Israel believes itself to have been *defiled* (see Genesis 34:5, 27). The reaction of Jacob's sons causes further disruption and disagreement within the covenant family. Now, God calls Jacob on another journey, one that will purify the community and reaffirm its special identity as the covenant family.

The members of Jacob's household are to *put away* (NRSV; NIV = *Get rid of*) their attachments to foreign gods. This is symbolized by getting rid of any idols they may have (see, for example, Genesis 31:19, 33-35) and any pieces of jewelry that are used as magical charms. They also may wash themselves (*purify yourselves*) before

106   GENESIS

putting on new clothes as an outward symbol of their inward resolve.

Verses 5-8: Jacob and his family escape retaliation for their deeds at Shechem (see Genesis 34:25-31) because of God's providential care. A *terror from God* is a panic that immobilizes or confuses the enemy (see also Exodus 23:27). God had appeared to Jacob at Bethel approximately thirty years before (see Genesis 28:10-19). Jacob now commemorates that revelation by building an altar and calling it *El-bethel* (*God of Bethel*).

It is unclear why this notice about Deborah's death appears here (see also Genesis 24:59). Rebekah's death is not reported, but Genesis 49:31 states that she was buried in the cave at Mach-pelah with Isaac and his parents.

Verses 9-15: God comes to Jacob to change his name and to bless him. The new name and the blessing have been given before (see also the comments on Genesis 28:12-14; 32:22-30). This text reaffirms Jacob's new identity and his special relationship with God Almighty. The covenant that God made with Abraham and Isaac (see also Genesis 12:1-7; 17:16; 26:2-4) is continued with Jacob. Jacob responds once again by setting up a memorial pillar and consecrating it to God with offerings of wine (*drink offering*) and oil. *Bethel* means *house of God*.

Verses 16-21: Jacob endures the loss of his beloved Rachel but has the joy of another son. *Benoni* means *son of my sorrow*. *Benjamin* means *son of the right hand* (that is, of the favored side). Despite his sorrow, Jacob (Israel) journeys on.

Verses 22-26: For reasons that are not explained, Reuben commits adultery with Bilhah, Jacob's concubine. This is not just an act of passion, but is an attempt by Reuben to gain power over Jacob or to take his father's place as head of the family (see also 2 Samuel 16:20-23). Because of his actions, Reuben loses his birthright and is condemned by Jacob (see Genesis 49:3-4; 1 Chronicles 5:1). The twelve sons of Jacob become the ancestors of the tribes of Israel (see also, for example, Deuteronomy 27:11-13).

The tradition behind this list understands that Benjamin was, like his brothers, born in Paddan-aram during Jacob's exile (see Genesis 29:31–30:24). Another tradition (verses 16-21) records that Benjamin was born in Canaan.

Verses 27-29: Jacob and Esau bury Isaac in the cave at Hebron that was purchased by Abraham (see Genesis 23:17-20; 49:31). The two brothers have gone their separate ways, but they are at peace with one another and are as one in honoring their father (see also Isaac and Ishmael; Genesis 25:7-10).

The Descendants of Esau (36:1-43)

Though not an heir to the promises of Abraham and Isaac that are passed on to Jacob, Esau is nevertheless important as a son and brother of the covenant family. This material testifies to the fertility, prosperity, and political power that Esau and his descendants find in their homeland of Edom. Though there will be struggles between Israel and Edom in the future, the biblical record is careful to maintain the close connection between Esau and Jacob and the nations that they found (see also Deuteronomy 23:7).

§ § § § § § §

The Message of Genesis 33–36

This part of Jacob's story shows us that the call to be in relationship with God does not exclude other relationships. Jacob and the covenant family must still live with one another and with the rest of the world, despite their differences. Esau is Jacob's brother but is still very different. The Canaanites are close neighbors but are also very different. Given the realities of these differences in everyday life, how is the covenant family supposed to live in the world?

§ The chosen people must maintain proper ritual and worship to affirm their faith and separate themselves from the worship of false gods.

§ The chosen people must recognize the special nature of God's call to them. They do not define their own identity. Rather, God calls them and gives them an identity in which their old ways and habits may not always apply (see also Ephesians 4:22-25; Hebrews 11:8-16).

§ The chosen people must trust God. They must accept the fact that they live in a world of life and death, of joy and grief, even as they continue their journey with God.

§ The covenant community must recognize that God is the God of all peoples. The stories about Esau, his reconciliation with Jacob, and his prosperity testify that God is also in relationship with him. We see that God cares for the chosen people in a special way but does not neglect the others. There are other sheep, that are not of this fold (see John 10:16).

§ § § § § § §

Genesis 37–40

Introduction to These Chapters

Chapters 37–50 form the last large section in the book
of Genesis. This section is introduced as *the story of the
family of Jacob* (Genesis 37:2), which continues the story
left off in Genesis 36:8. Most of this history focuses on
Joseph, the eldest son of Jacob and Rachel. Jacob's
favoritism toward Joseph causes his brothers to become
jealous, and this leads to Joseph being sold into slavery
in Egypt. Through his natural abilities and God's
providential care, Joseph survives and rises to a position
of great power in Egypt. This position in turn leads to a
reconciliation with his family and to their rescue from
famine in Canaan.

Here is an outline of Genesis 37–40.
I. Joseph Sold into Slavery (37:1-36)
II. Judah and Tamar (38:1-30)
III. Joseph in Potiphar's Household (39:1-23)
IV. Joseph in Prison (40:1-23)

Joseph Sold into Slavery (37:1-36)

From the time of God's call and promises to Abraham,
there has been conflict within the covenant family (see,
for example, Genesis 16:1-15; 27:1-46; 34:1-31). Jacob was
even in conflict with his brother before they were born
(see Genesis 25:22-26). Jacob's sons continue this
tradition as they scheme to get rid of Joseph.

Verses 1-11: Jacob (sometimes also called *Israel* as in

110

verse 3; see also Genesis 35:9-10) and his family are living in the area of Hebron in the hill country south of Jerusalem. They are prosperous, semi-nomadic stockbreeders. Joseph, like his half-brothers, had been born in Mesopotamia (see Genesis 30:1-24). He is not only the child of Jacob's old age, but is also the son of Rachel, who was Jacob's most loved wife.

The *long robe with sleeves* (NRSV), or *richly ornamented robe* (NIV) or *coat of many colors* (King James Version) is a gift of distinction that is more luxurious than the common knee-length tunic that is sleeveless. This gift sets Joseph apart as one especially chosen and honored.

In the Old Testament, and in the ancient Near East in general, dreams are in many cases understood as a means of communication between humans and the divine (see also, for example, Genesis 28:12-17; Daniel 2:17-45). Joseph's two dreams symbolize future events from his life in Egypt (see Genesis 42:6-9; 50:18). His brothers and father see clearly enough that the dreams picture them humbling themselves before Joseph. None of them, however, yet understand the full meaning. Joseph will himself go through many humbling experiences and years of hard work and uncertainty before he receives this honor from his family.

Traditionally, it is the oldest son who receives from his father the honor and leadership of the family. Jacob, however, took the place of his older brother in the family order (see Genesis 25:23-34; 27:35-36), and Joseph is destined to be the leader among his brothers.

Verses 12-28: Joseph seeks his brothers at Shechem north of Jerusalem where Jacob owns land (see Genesis 33:18-20) but finds them at Dothan in a valley a few miles to the north. They decide to get rid of him and of his dreams, which are threatening to them. The *pit* (verse 20) is a dry cistern.

Some scholars believe that two different traditions are combined in these verses to explain how Joseph is sold into slavery. In one tradition, Reuben seeks to rescue Joseph from the pit, but he has already been kidnapped by passing Midianite traders. In another tradition, the brothers agree to sell him to Ishmaelite traders. As the story now stands, Reuben's attempts to save Joseph are spoiled when the Midianites capture Joseph and sell him before Reuben or the other brothers can get to him.

The brothers decide not to kill Joseph not only because he is of their *own flesh*, but also because his spilled blood could not be concealed. The blood would *cry out* from the ground against the injustice done (see Genesis 4:8-12).

Verses 29-36: Jacob, who once deceived his own father (see Genesis 27:1-29), is now deceived by his sons. He goes through the traditional mourning rituals but is not comforted by them or by his other children. He wants to die and join Joseph in Sheol, the world of the dead. Sheol (also called the Pit) is seen not as a happy place but as a shadowy world in which there is little comfort and where one is not in full relationship with God.

Judah and Tamar (38:1-30)

This chapter leaves the story of Joseph to focus on his brother Judah. This episode in Judah's life explains the birth of his son, Perez, who becomes the ancestor of King David (see Ruth 4:18-22).

Verses 1-11: At the same time that Joseph is sold into slavery, Judah moves to Adullam, west of Hebron, and marries a Canaanite woman. His daughter-in-law, Tamar, is probably also a Canaanite. Tamar has a right to expect another husband from Judah's family after Er and Onan die. According to ancient marriage law, a brother is obligated to marry his brother's widow so that the dead man may have descendants. In this way the dead brother's name and inheritance will be maintained (see also Deuteronomy 25:5-10; Ruth 4:1-8). Judah does not understand that Er and Onan died because of their wickedness. He fears that Tamar may have something to do with their deaths, so he sends her back to her father's home, falsely promising her that Shelah will one day be her husband.

Verses 12-19: When Tamar realizes Judah has lied to her, she takes matters into her own hands. The urge and need for children is strong in ancient society because children are believed to be blessings from God and because of the security and honor that come from having children (see also the story of Lot's daughters in Genesis 19:30-38).

The *signet* (NRSV; NIV = *seal*) that Tamar requires from Judah as a guarantee that he will pay her is a seal that is hung on a cord. Such a seal is used to stamp a signature into clay or wax and is a very personal form of identification.

Verses 20-26: Judah thinks that he has found a common prostitute, but his friend asks in town for a woman whom he thinks is a cult prostitute. Cult prostitutes often work in association with a pagan shrine and have ritual sexual intercourse as part of fertility rites (see also Deuteronomy 23:17-18).

Israelite law requires either stoning or burning for those caught in harlotry or adultery. Tamar's life is spared because Judah confesses his guilt in the whole situation. Her right to have children by her husband's family justifies her actions. To be *righteous* is to be in right relationship to God. Even though Tamar is a Canaanite, she is recognized as a righteous one in comparison to Judah, who is a member of the covenant family.

Verses 27-30: Perez means *a breach,* and *Zerah* means *brightness,* perhaps referring to the red thread tied around his hand. Because Tamar is righteous (verse 26), her children become part of the covenant family. Perez will become the ancestor of King David and of Jesus (see Ruth 4:18-22; 1 Chronicles 2:4; Matthew 1:3).

Joseph in Potiphar's Household (39:1-23)

Though Joseph must now live as a slave instead of as an honored son, God has not abandoned him. God's care for Joseph is evident even though he ends up in prison.

Verses 1-6: Potiphar is a high official serving in Pharaoh's court, possibly having authority over the royal prison. Like his father before him, Joseph brings prosperity and success to the man he serves (see also Genesis 30:25-30). Potiphar may not recognize that it is the Lord who blesses him through Joseph, but he does recognize the benefits he enjoys because of Joseph's abilities. He maintains personal control only over his food, probably because of Egyptian dietary laws that forbid eating with foreigners (see Genesis 43:32).

Joseph makes the most of his situation and becomes a model administrator. He is hard-working, honest, loyal to his owner, and righteous before God.

Verses 7-18: This story is similar to an ancient Egyptian story called *Tale of Two Brothers*, though the exact connections between the two stories, if any, are not clear. The tale is about a man who rejects the advances of his brother's wife, who then falsely accuses him of forcing himself on her. The innocent man barely escapes with his life.

The term *Hebrew* (verses 14, 17) is applied to the people of Israel in the Old Testament when they are speaking of themselves to non-Israelites or when non-Israelites are speaking of them. More commonly they call themselves *Israelites*.

The relationship between the Israelites/Hebrews and other peoples of this time called the *'Apiru* or *Hapiru* is a matter of dispute. The 'Apiru/Hapiru are mentioned in texts from other ancient Near Eastern societies, but no direct connection has been established between them and the Israelites.

The 'Apiru were perhaps a class of people rather than an ethnic group. They appear to have been a class of people who lived without direct citizenship and without a permanent place within existing societies. This description fits the Israelites at this stage of their history, especially since it is known from Egyptian documents that 'Apiru peoples were among the slaves who served Pharaoh Rameses II (1290–1224 B.C.).

Verses 19-23: Joseph prospers even in prison because of God's care. This is not to say that his life is easy. He is still a slave and must see to the needs of others (see Genesis 40:4), and he is certainly not free to leave the dungeon. Yet, God's purposes are at work in Joseph's life.

Joseph in Prison (40:1-23)

Joseph is unjustly confined to prison and must serve others even in his captivity. He is still under God's care, however, and is a channel of God's wisdom to others.

Verses 1-8: The prison is considered as part of Potiphar's *house* (verses 3, 7). Joseph is still treated as a slave who must see to the needs of the other prisoners.

In ancient times, dreams were believed to be channels of communication between humans and the divine. Dreams were also believed to be means of knowing the future (see, for example, Genesis 37:5-11; Daniel 2). There were, in some ancient societies, officials who specialized in interpreting dreams for their king. In some cases, elaborate dream books were compiled that listed many dreams from the past and the events that followed them. These books were used to help the interpreters understand new dreams.

Joseph clearly rejects these methods of interpretation. He declares that God alone provides such wisdom. The implication is that God sent the dreams so only God can truly interpret them. Joseph also assumes the responsibility for being a channel of God's messages to the butler and baker.

Verses 9-19: The butler will be *lifted up* (verse 13) and restored to his former honored position. The baker will not be so fortunate. His head will literally be *lifted up* (verse 19) off his shoulders and his body impaled as carrion for the birds. The justice or injustice of all this is not explained. All these events happen by Pharaoh's will.

Pharaoh also has the power to save Joseph from prison. Joseph appeals to the butler to remember the kindness Joseph has shown him and to plead Joseph's case before Pharaoh.

Verses 20-23: The butler forgets Joseph and does nothing to help him. Despite his wisdom and faithfulness, Joseph must wait. God has more dreams for the Egyptians, however, and has not forgotten Joseph (see Genesis 41).

§ § § § § § §

The Message of Genesis 37–40

The story of Joseph is like a short novel with elements of suspense, intrigue, misfortune, mystery, and love. We see the family of Jacob living in a very real world of family conflicts and natural calamities that dramatically affect their lives. Working in and through all of this, however, is the overriding purpose and will of God. What does Joseph's story tell us about God's activity in the world?

§ The storyteller never lets the reader forget that God is the key player in all of this, even though God's presence is not always clearly seen.

§ Human failings and frailties cannot be denied, but they do not determine the final outcome in the history of the covenant family.

§ Like the stories of the patriarchs before it, the story of Joseph shows us the further working out of God's purposes in the world. Other people in the world who come in contact with the chosen people can be blessed by their presence.

§ § § § § § §

PART SIXTEEN Genesis 41–43

Introduction to These Chapters

In these chapters Joseph rises to a position of great power in Egypt and comes in contact with his family once again.

These three chapters may be outlined as follows.
I. Joseph Interprets Pharaoh's Dreams (41:1-57)
II. Joseph's Brothers Come to Egypt (42:1-38)
III. Joseph's Brothers Return to Egypt (43:1-34)

Joseph Interprets Pharaoh's Dreams (41:1-57)

Through the power and influence of God, Joseph interprets Pharaoh's dreams and becomes the architect of a plan to deal with the coming famine. Joseph not only improves his own position but also saves countless lives because of his God-given wisdom.

The exact identity of this Pharaoh is still a matter of debate. The text itself and historical records from outside the Bible, however, provide a few clues about the general time and circumstances of this Pharaoh and Joseph. From 1730–1570 B.C. a group of Pharaohs known as the Hyksos Dynasty ruled Egypt. They were not native Egyptians but were foreign rulers from parts of Mesopotamia, which is where Joseph's ancestors were from. It is much more likely that a non-Egyptian such as Joseph would gain a prominent place in Egyptian government under such a ruler than under a native Egyptian ruler.

Joseph's family is eventually invited to come live *near*

him in the Nile delta region in northern Egypt (see Genesis 45:10). As Pharaoh's chief minister, Joseph would live and work in the capital city, which was in the delta region during the Hyksos period.

None of this evidence is conclusive nor does it narrow the choice to one particular pharaoh, but it does perhaps give a general time frame for Joseph's story.

Verses 1-8: God communicates not only with believers but also with nonbelievers through dreams (see, for example, Genesis 20:1-7; Daniel 2; 4). In this case, God is sending a famine on the land (see verse 31) but is giving Pharaoh a warning of the coming disaster.

The Nile River is the source of fertility in Egypt. The annual flooding of the river not only brings water to the dry land but also deposits rich soil on the fields that maintains their fertility. Seasonal rains in the tropical highlands to the south of Egypt cause the river to rise and flood the land as it flows northward to the Mediterranean Sea. Years of decreased rainfall in the south would bring drought and famine in the north.

Cattle breeding was important in Egypt, and many ancient Egyptian paintings show people caring for cattle. Specimens of a multi-eared strain of wheat have been found in mummy cases, and such varieties of grain are still grown in Egypt. The *east wind* that blights the grain in Pharaoh's dream is the sirocco, a hot, dry wind that blows off the eastern desert during the summer months.

Verses 9-24: Joseph proves himself to be a faithful, humble servant of God. Though he has been serving his Egyptian masters all this time, he has access to a power and wisdom far greater than any they possess (compare verse 8 and verse 16).

Verses 25-36: Joseph tells Pharaoh that both the famine and the dreams are from God (verse 32). He then not only interprets the dreams but also recommends a plan to save food for the coming lean years so that the people *may survive* (verses 33-36).

All of Pharaoh's great powers and the wisdom of his so-called *wise men* are not enough to meet this crisis. It will take a man who is discreet (discerning) and wise in the ways of God to handle the situation. The story gives no hint that Joseph is deliberately describing himself here. He presents himself to Pharaoh only as the channel of God's word.

The Egyptian people will be required to give one-fifth of their crops to the government for the next seven years. The government will store the food to be used during the seven years of famine.

Verses 37-45: Pharaoh acknowledges Joseph's God-given wisdom and makes him second-in-command in Egypt. The powers given him are like that of vizier, an office that is known from ancient Egyptian records. A man named Rekh-mi-Re held such an office during the reign of Pharaoh Thut-mose II (1490–1435 B.C.).

The signet ring, fine linen clothes, gold chain, and chariot are symbols of Joseph's new office. The Hebrew words that are here translated *signet ring, fine linen,* and *bow the knee* (NRSV; NIV = *make way*) all originally come from Egyptian words. The horse and chariot were first used in Egypt during the Hyksos period.

Joseph also receives an Egyptian name as a mark of his transition into a position of trust and power in Egyptian society. This name perhaps means *God speaks: he lives.* Joseph's father-in-law, Potiphera, is a priest in the city of On, northeast of Cairo. On is the center of worship for the Egyptian sun god, Ra.

Verses 46-57: Joseph has now been in Egypt thirteen years (see Genesis 37:2-3). He flourishes in his government position and in his family life. Though God sends the famine, God also sends the means to cope with it. The benefits of Joseph's wisdom extend beyond the borders of Egypt to all the surrounding countries. At other times in the past, Egypt has also served as a storehouse for hungry neighbors (see Genesis 12:10).

Joseph is also *fruitful* and is compensated for his years of affliction by the birth of his sons. *Manasseh* means *making to forget*. *Ephraim* means *to be fruitful*.

Joseph's Brothers Come to Egypt (42:1-38)

In this chapter the storyteller begins to reveal another side of Joseph. He is now a powerful man, not a helpless boy or a slave as in the past. In his new identity and his new position of authority he is suddenly confronted with his brothers and with his past. No doubt Joseph has strong, conflicting feelings about all this, including both joy and anger. In order to resolve the situation, Joseph uses his power to manipulate his brothers and to deceive them. His primary concern is to see his brother, Benjamin, and so his determination to see Benjamin comes into conflict with Jacob's determination to keep Benjamin safely with him.

Verses 1-5: Egyptian documents and artwork show that people from famine-stricken countries came to Egypt for food even before Joseph's time (see also Genesis 12:10).

Verses 6-17: Joseph speaks Egyptian to his brothers and uses an interpreter (see verse 23). They do not recognize him because he is now a grown man who speaks and dresses as an Egyptian. They think Joseph is dead (*is no more*, verse 13).

Joseph remembers the dreams he had about them when he was a boy (see Genesis 37:1-11) in which his brothers symbolically bowed down before him. He also probably guesses that these dreams are what prompted them to get rid of him (see Genesis 37:19-20). Thus, he speaks harshly to them, and they do indeed bow down to him and humble themselves before him. Joseph accuses them of being spies who have come to see whether Egypt is vulnerable to attack. Through the centuries Egypt faced many invasions from the east, so this charge does not sound completely outlandish.

Joseph swears an oath by the life of Pharaoh that the

brothers will stay in prison until the younger brother is sent to Egypt as proof of their innocence. The assumption behind this oath is perhaps that no father would risk the lives of all his sons on such a dangerous mission. Thus, having all the brothers in Egypt would prove that their motives are honorable.

By putting them in prison, Joseph is also giving them a taste of what he had to endure for many years.

Verses 18-25: Because Joseph fears God, he must abide by God's standard of justice. He cannot justly punish these men without proof of their guilt, so he compromises with them. They, in the meantime, have had a chance to reflect on their situation and are beginning to understand the connection between what is happening to them now and what they did to Joseph years ago. They ignored his pleas for mercy and ignored Reuben's argument that they were committing a sin against an innocent boy. The shedding of innocent blood is a crime that cannot be concealed forever, and it must be reckoned for (see also Genesis 4:8-11; 37:26).

Joseph realizes that they recognize their crime against him, so he arranges for them to go home not only with grain but with their money as well.

Verses 26-38: The discovery of the money (verse 28) gives the brothers their first clue that God has a hand in what is happening to them. They do not see it as a good omen, however, but believe that it is somehow part of God's retribution on them for their treatment of Joseph. They may fear that when they return to reclaim their brother, Simeon, they will be accused of stealing as well as spying (verse 35).

Jacob will not agree to let them take Benjamin to Egypt, even with Reuben's promise to exchange the lives of his sons for Simeon and Benjamin. Jacob sees this as another disaster that his sons have brought to him. They brought him the news of Joseph's (supposed) death years before and now they tell him that Simeon is a hostage in

Egypt. Jacob declares that also losing Benjamin would kill him.

This is not to be the last word, however, for God is still at work and God's purposes for Jacob's family will be fulfilled.

Joseph's Brothers Return to Egypt (43:1-34)

Continuing famine forces Jacob to relent and to allow his older sons to take Benjamin with them to Egypt so they may get more food. He resigns himself to face the possible loss of his sons.

Verses 1-15: These verses show that this final version of Joseph's story may have been put together from more than one source of tradition (see also the Introduction on pages 7-10). In some parts of the story, Joseph's father is called *Jacob* (for example, chapter 42). In this chapter, however, he is called *Israel* (see also Genesis 35:9-10). In another part of the story, Reuben bargains with Jacob so they may return to Egypt with Benjamin (see Genesis 42:37). In chapter 43 Judah bargains with Israel. Parts of Joseph's conversation with his brothers are revealed here (verse 7) that are not mentioned in chapter 42 (see 42:9-16). In chapter 43, verse 21 says that the brothers find all their money in their sacks on their way home. In chapter 42, they find part of the money on the way and the rest after they arrive home (verses 26-35).

All this confusion shows that the story of Joseph was told and retold by many people through the years before this final version was put together. The people who put the different strands of the story together to make the version we have today did not smooth over or eliminate details in the text that do not exactly match. They must have believed that each strand was important and that each contributed to the truth and message of the story.

Verses 16-25: It is probably unusual for high Egyptian officials to entertain foreigners who come to Egypt seeking food. Joseph's brothers are still wary of him because of their encounter with him on their first visit, and his hospitality prompts them to try to explain their predicament to one of Joseph's servants.

The servant does not tell them that Joseph had their money put back in their sacks (see Genesis 42:25). He does, however, try to put them at ease by telling them that God has a hand in what is happening to them. This is the major theme that is repeated throughout the story of Joseph: God is at work in human events even though we may not always realize it (see also, for example, Genesis 39:5, 23; 50:20).

Verses 26-34: The brothers still do not catch on to their situation, despite all the unusual things that have been happening to them. Joseph, though overcome with emotion at seeing his beloved brother Benjamin, continues to deceive his brothers.

Joseph eats apart from his brothers because of his great rank. The Egyptians who share the meal eat apart from everyone else because of class and religious distinctions (see also Genesis 39:6).

Though he is the youngest, Benjamin is treated as the most honored guest. Serving a special dish of meat is also a traditional way of honoring someone at a feast. Though the brothers make merry at Joseph's table and are perhaps reassured by their good treatment, Joseph is not yet through manipulating them to get what he wants (see Genesis 44).

§ § § § § § §

The Message of Genesis 41–43

The story of Joseph shows us human nature both at its best and at its worst. We are not given an idealized picture of the covenant family but are allowed to see them as people of the real world who are sometimes caught in difficult circumstances and who are sometimes at odds with one another. The most important thing about them, however, is their relationship with God, and how they live within that relationship. This relationship is not always as smooth or as strong as it could be, however. What does this story tell us about their feelings and actions toward one another and about their personal relationship to God?

§ Joseph is wise and discerning but also manipulative and deceptive. At times he is overcome by feelings of both joy and anxiety. Above all, he is open to God's revelation.

§ Joseph's brothers are jealous, angry, heartless, and deceptive. Later they are stricken with guilt and believe that God's judgment has finally caught up with them. Even in the midst of this situation, however, they can find reasons to be merry.

§ Jacob is fearful and resigned to grief, though later he has reason to rejoice.

This story thus reveals the strong and often conflicting emotions that influence the lives of Jacob and his sons. How does God work into all this?

§ God works through people, through their weaknesses as well as their strengths, to accomplish God's divine purposes for the world.

§ God is greater than the strongest earthly power.

§ God rules the natural world.

§ God's wisdom is available to human beings who are open and responsive.

§ God's wisdom and power are greater than any human wisdom or power.

§ § § § § § §

PART SEVENTEEN Genesis 44–47

Introduction to These Chapters

In these chapters, Joseph is finally reconciled with his brothers and is reunited with his father, Jacob.

Here is an outline of Genesis 44–47.
I. The Final Test of Joseph's Brothers (44:1-34)
II. Reconciliation (45:1-28)
III. Jacob's Migration to Egypt (46:1-34)
IV. The Family of Jacob Prospers in Egypt (47:1-26)
V. The Death of Jacob (47:27-31)

The Final Test of Joseph's Brothers (44:1-34)

Joseph continues to deceive his brothers so that they think they are once again in peril. On the one hand, it seems that Joseph would like to keep Benjamin in Egypt with him but would let the others go back to Canaan. This is not his final goal, however. The situation he sets up will show him whether or not his brothers have changed. Will they sacrifice Benjamin for their own benefit as they had sacrificed Joseph years ago? After all, their father obviously loves Benjamin very much and favored his mother over their own mothers. Even in Egypt Benjamin has been shown favor over them (see Genesis 43:34).

Joseph receives an answer to his questions from his brother Judah: The brothers will not abandon Benjamin nor cause their father further grief.

Verses 1-13: The *silver cup* is used to tell the future. In Egypt and in Mesopotamia magical rituals were performed by pouring oil or water into special bowls and then foretelling future events by the appearance of the liquids.

The brothers point to their past honesty (see Genesis 43:12) as evidence in their favor when they are accused of stealing Joseph's cup. They condemn themselves to death or slavery if they are found guilty. When they realize the seriousness of their situation, they tear their clothes as people do in mourning.

Verses 14-34: Joseph leads his brothers to believe that he found out about their crime through divination. Judah then speaks for the group and offers all of them as slaves, even Benjamin (compare verse 9). Their guilt has been exposed, not only in this present case but also their guilt in how they treated Joseph so many years before (see also Genesis 42:22).

In verse 17, Joseph sets up the real test: Will the brothers save themselves and sacrifice Benjamin?

Judah's reply in verses 18-34 summarizes what has happened since the brothers first came to Egypt. He tries to get Joseph to see his own part in all of this and to understand the consequences for Benjamin's father if the boy does not return home. As a final gesture of good faith, Judah offers to take Benjamin's place as Joseph's slave.

Reconciliation (45:1-28)

This chapter brings a joyful resolution to the conflicts that began so long ago.

Verses 1-15: The brothers are dumbfounded by Joseph's first confession to them. His explanation to them in verses 5-8 contains the central message of this story: God is behind everything that has happened to them (see also Genesis 50:20). God used Joseph's slavery and rise to power in Egypt as a way of saving his family. Jacob, his children, and his grandchildren are a *remnant*, or small group of people who have been chosen by God to carry on the promises made to Abraham (see, for example, Genesis 12:1-7; 50:24). Their *survivors* are the covenant family that will eventually grow into the people of Israel.

Joseph is *a father to Pharaoh*, that is, the chief minister to Pharaoh. Because of his position of power, he can invite all his family to come live in Egypt and enjoy the benefits of this land. The land of *Goshen* is a fertile region in the northeastern Nile delta.

Verses 16-28: Though generous and forgiving with all his brothers, Joseph still favors Benjamin and gives him the most gifts. His instructions to his brothers not to *quarrel* (verse 24) clearly show how Joseph has now become the leader in his family. There is also no question that they will come live under his protection in Egypt.

The story does not say how the brothers explain to Jacob why Joseph is not dead but is alive. Perhaps Jacob's happiness allows him to forgive his sons' past crimes and deceptions.

Jacob's Migration to Egypt (46:1-34)

Jacob and Joseph are reunited, and God's past promises concerning Jacob's family are renewed.

Verses 1-7: Jacob leaves Hebron and stops at Beersheba, which is the southern limit of Canaan, on his way to Egypt. At Beersheba God appeared to Isaac, blessed him, and promised him many descendants (see Genesis 26:23-25). Isaac built a shrine there in memorial to this revelation, and it is here that Jacob stops to make his sacrifices before leaving Canaan.

God comes to Jacob/Israel (see Genesis 32:28; 35:10) in *visions of the night* (see also Daniel 2:19). These are not ordinary dreams but are visions of divine revelation. In these visions God reassures Jacob that God's past promises to him will be fulfilled (see Genesis 28:10-17) even though Jacob is leaving the Promised Land. God promises Jacob that the divine presence will be with him, even in a foreign land. Jacob will also have the comfort of knowing that he and Joseph will be together until Jacob's death (*shall close your eyes*).

God will bring Jacob himself out of Egypt only after his death when his body will be returned to Canaan (see Genesis 50:1-7). God will also symbolically bring Jacob out of Egypt when his descendants are delivered from slavery many generations later (see also Genesis 15:13-14).

Verses 8-27: This genealogy lists the members of Jacob's family who migrate to Egypt (see also Exodus 1:1-5). They are the ancestors of the tribes of Israel that will later leave Egypt under the leadership of Moses (see Numbers 26).

Verses 28-34: Joseph is perhaps afraid that Pharaoh will not welcome his family in Egypt once the king knows that they are shepherds. He seeks to arrange for them to settle in the northeastern delta region of the country (*Goshen*). Herdsmen are apparently tolerated in these outlying areas, and the family will also be closer to Joseph here (see Genesis 45:10). The reasons why the Egyptians dislike herdsmen are unclear. Perhaps the out-of-door life led by the shepherds is looked upon as rough and unclean by the Egyptians. Perhaps also it is sheep-breeders and not cattle-breeders that the Egyptians object to because the Egyptians themselves kept large herds of cattle (see Genesis 47:6).

The Family of Jacob Prospers in Egypt (47:1-26)

Once Jacob's family is safely settled in Egypt, the story turns its attention to Joseph's program for handling the continuing famine. Despite the hard times in the land, Jacob's family has grown and prospered by the time of his death.

Verses 1-12: Pharaoh grants the brothers' request to be allowed to settle in Goshen, and in return asks to receive help from them with his own cattle herds.

Jacob blesses or pays respect to Pharaoh, probably wishing him the customary prosperity, security, and long life. In Jacob's view, his life is short compared to that of his father, Isaac (who lived 180 years), and his grandfather, Abraham (who lived 175 years). He believes that his life has been hard and full of *evil* for he has been in conflict with his father and brother (see Genesis 27), with his father-in-law (see Genesis 31), and with his sons (see Genesis 37).

The *land of Rameses* is a later name for the land of Goshen. Rameses is the royal name used by a later generation of Pharaohs.

Verses 13-26: As the famine drags on the people grow more desperate for food and eventually become tenant farmers on their land. Pharaoh now owns the land and provides the seed for crops. The people pay a fifth of their produce in tax and keep the rest for themselves. Only religious property is exempt.

Egyptian historical records state that such a system of land management was introduced there sometime between 1700–1500 B.C. The writers of this part of Joseph's story say that this was still the situation in Egypt in their day.

Despite the fact that they now work for Pharaoh, the people believe that they are better off than before. They praise Joseph for saving their lives.

The Death of Jacob (47:27-31)

Israel (verse 27) means the people of Israel, Jacob's family. Just as Abraham, Isaac, and Jacob before them, they prosper in a foreign land (see also Genesis 12:17–13:2; 26:6-13; 31:17-18).

On his deathbed Jacob/Israel asks Joseph to swear an oath that he will see that Jacob is buried in his ancestral tomb in Canaan. This is the tomb that Abraham bought (see Genesis 23:17-20) and it is the resting place of Jacob's parents and grandparents (see Genesis 49:31-32).

(Concerning the significance of Jacob's request to Joseph to *put your hand under my thigh,* see the comments on Genesis 24:1-9.)

The exact translation and meaning of *Israel bowed himself on the head of his bed* (NRSV; NIV = *worshiped as he leaned on the top of his staff*) is still a matter of debate. The general idea seems to be that Jacob bows his head in gratitude and relief that Joseph has sworn to carry out his request.

§ § § § § § §

The Message of Genesis 44–47

Sometimes even those people who are in relationship with God cannot immediately see the ways of God in everything that happens to them. In Joseph's case, it took years for him to understand the full significance of his slavery and exile from his family. With the coming of his brothers to Egypt, he finally saw how God's purposes were being fulfilled in his life. What does Joseph's life tell us about God's purposes and how they are fulfilled?

§ God's purposes in the world are saving purposes.

§ God can bring good out of evil, life out of death.

§ God works through people to accomplish these purposes.

§ The covenant family has been chosen to play a special role in God's plan for the world. In this case, Joseph saves not only the lives of his family but of thousands of other people as well.

§ God's saving purposes include not only spiritual necessities (an abiding relationship with God Almighty) but physical necessities as well (food, water, and a safe place to live).

§ God's purposes for the covenant family do not end in Egypt. Many survivors will bear God's promises and purposes into the future.

§ § § § § § §

Genesis 48–50

Introduction to These Chapters

The book of Genesis ends with the deaths of Jacob and Joseph. In these three chapters, relationships among the members of the covenant family are defined and future roles are revealed. All of this looks toward the future, toward the day when the family of Jacob will leave Egypt as a great multitude of people and will establish themselves in the Promised Land.

Here is an outline of chapters 48–50.
   I. Jacob Adopts and Blesses Joseph's Sons (48:1-22)
  II. Jacob's Farewell Address (49:1-33)
 III. The Burial of Jacob (50:1-21)
 IV. The Death of Joseph (50:22-26)

Jacob Adopts and Blesses Joseph's Sons (48:1-22)

Jacob adopts Joseph's half-Egyptian sons (see Genesis 41:46-52) into the covenant family.

Verses 1-7: Jacob tells Joseph about God coming to him at Bethel (Luz) and granting him the same promises made to Abraham and Isaac (see Genesis 12–22). As Jacob's adopted sons, Ephraim and Manasseh will now become heirs of those promises. Any other children Joseph has will be considered part of the families of Ephraim and Manasseh. Thus, all of Joseph's children will inherit the promises given by God to the covenant family.

Reuben and Simeon are Jacob's oldest sons, born to

Leah (see Genesis 29:31-33). Since Rachel died while giving birth to Benjamin (see Genesis 35:16-20), Jacob can no longer have children by her. Thus he claims their grandsons as his own sons.

Verses 8-14: Joseph brings his sons next to Jacob for the formal adoption ceremony. He puts Manasseh, the older son, on Jacob's right hand and Ephraim on his left because the right side is considered the favorable and honored side. Jacob, however, crosses his hands so that his right hand is on Ephraim's head.

Verses 15-22: A deathbed blessing is especially strong (see also the comments on Genesis 27 concerning the power of blessings). In his blessing, Jacob recalls God's redeeming actions on his behalf in the past. God was with his fathers (see Genesis 17:1; 24:40) and was likewise his shepherd (*led me*) through good times and bad. The *angel* of God came to him in times of trial (see Genesis 28:10-17; 32:1-2, 22-30).

The descendants of Ephraim and Manasseh grow to be powerful tribes in Israel, both of whom eventually settle in the central hill country of Canaan. The tribe of Ephraim, however, eventually becomes stronger and more prominent than the tribe of Manasseh. In later generations, the Northern Kingdom of Israel was sometimes called *Ephraim* (see, for example, Isaiah 11:13; Ezekiel 37:16).

The future prosperity and fertility of the tribes of Ephraim and Manasseh will become the standard by which the people of Israel will bless one another (verse 20).

It is not only Ephraim but also Joseph himself who receives a blessing usually given an older son (verse 22). The *ridge of land* (NIV; NRSV = *portion*) may refer to the city or area of Shechem in what will later become the territory of Ephraim. Elsewhere in Genesis, Jacob is said to have had peaceful dealings with Shechem (see Genesis 33:18-20). It is his sons who take up arms against the city (see Genesis 34:25-29).

Jacob's Farewell Address (49:1-33)

In this poem, Jacob addresses his sons not just as individuals but also as the tribes they will become. He speaks to them of the future (*what will happen to you in days to come*) when their descendants will be living in the Promised Land. In general, the poem reflects the situation of the Israelite tribes during the reign of King David (1000–961 B.C.).

Verses 1-4: Jacob turns to the past to explain Reuben's future. Though granted all the benefits of a firstborn son, Reuben slept with his father's concubine and thus forfeited his rights (see the comments on Genesis 35:22). Reuben's tribe settled east of the Jordan River and was eventually absorbed into Moab.

Verses 5-7: Simeon and Levi are cursed for their vengeful attack on the city of Shechem (see Genesis 34:25-31). The tribe of Simeon received relatively little territory in Canaan and was absorbed into the tribe of Judah. Levi became the priestly class in Israel. In verse 7, *Jacob* and *Israel* refer to the nation of Israel, the descendants of Jacob.

Verses 8-12: Judah now receives the blessing denied to his older brothers. The tribe of Judah will become the dominant tribe in Israel. They took a leading role in the conquest of Canaan and controlled the territory around Jerusalem, the capital city of Israel under David and Solomon.

The strength of Judah is symbolized by the lion. This strength is both military and political for the tribe of Judah became a tribe of rulers. Both Jews and Christians also interpret verse 10 as a reference to the messiah who will come from Judah and will rule over all peoples. Jesus was born into this tribe and was later called *the Lion of the tribe of Judah* (see Revelation 5:5).

Verses 11-12 tell that the vineyards and pasture lands of Judah will produce great bounty.

Verse 13: The territory of Zebulun gave them access to

the Mediterranean Sea near the Phoenician port city of Sidon (see also Deuteronomy 33:18-19).

Verses 14-15: Issachar's territory included parts of Galilee and the fertile plain of Jezreel. Though robust and blessed with a pleasant land, this tribe was never completely independent from the Canaanite neighbors who lived in their midst.

Verses 16-18: Dan (which means *he judged*) governs or gets justice for his people. Dan was a small tribe that retained its vigor and independence despite pressure on its territory from the Philistines. This tribe will be a *viper* to its enemies.

The relationship of verse 18 to verses 16-17 is uncertain. Verse 18 may be a short prayer that was originally at some other place in the poem but was misplaced here during the transmission of the text. This prayer may perhaps be related to the difficulties the tribe of Dan will have with its enemies. Because of their trouble, they pray and wait for God's help.

Verse 19: The tribe of Gad settled east of the Jordan River in Gilead north of the territory of Reuben. This tribe was attacked by Ammonite raiders, but it successfully defended itself (see also Judges 11).

Verse 20: The tribe of Asher settled along the Mediterranean coast between Mount Carmel and Phoenicia. This rich, fertile land was very productive, and Asher was famous for its production of olive oil (see also Deuteronomy 33:24).

Verse 21: The tribe of Naphtali settled in a fertile region between the Mediterranean coastal lands and the Sea of Galilee. Naphtali is compared to a *doe,* a strong, agile, yet wild creature who produces beautiful offspring.

Verses 22-26: Joseph receives this blessing, though his descendants are later divided into the tribes of Ephraim and Manasseh.

Joseph is compared to a fruitful tree. *His branches* are Ephraim and Manasseh. These tribes grew strong and prospered in the hill country of Canaan despite the Canaanite *archers* who opposed them (see also Joshua 17:17-18). All of this happens by the will and power of God. The *Mighty One of Jacob* is *the God of your father*.

God will provide the house of Joseph with prosperity and fertility. The *blessings of heaven* are the rain and sunshine. The *blessings of the deep* are springs of water from the earth. The *blessings of the breasts and of the womb* include both children and flocks.

The exact translation of verse 26 is still a matter of debate. According to the NRSV translation, Jacob's blessing is mightier even than the natural strength and fertility that Joseph's descendants will find in the mountains of the Promised Land. Jacob passes the blessings of his ancestors received from God on to Joseph.

Joseph was *set apart from his brothers* for many years before they came to Egypt. Now he is *set apart* in that he is granted an honored position through the power of Jacob's blessing.

Verse 27: The tribe of Benjamin settled in the mountains between Jerusalem and Bethel. Though the tribe was small, the men of Benjamin were fierce warriors (see also Judges 20:14-16). King Saul (see 1 Samuel 9:1-2) and the apostle Paul (see Romans 11:1) were Benjaminites.

Verses 28-33: Concerning the purchase of the field and cave at Machpelah, see Genesis 23. Jacob now tells all his sons what he told Joseph (see Genesis 47:29-31): He wants to be buried with his ancestors in the Promised Land. With the address to his sons and the instructions concerning his burial completed, Jacob's earthly tasks are finished, and he dies.

The Burial of Jacob (50:1-21)

Verses 1-3: Jacob's body is embalmed so that it may be carried on the long journey to Canaan. Well-preserved Egyptian mummies from the time of Joseph are on display in museums even today. Among other embalming techniques, the body was soaked in a solution of salt and soda for forty or more days to preserve it from decay.

The Egyptians mourned for a dead king for seventy-two days. As a gesture of respect for Jacob, they mourn his death for seventy days.

Verses 4-14: Joseph receives permission to keep the oath that he swore to his father to bury Jacob in Canaan. Members of Pharaoh's court and several Egyptian dignitaries travel with Joseph's family to Canaan to pay their last respects to Jacob.

It is not clear why they travel east of (*beyond*) the Jordan River on their journey from Egypt to Canaan (verse 10). The main travel route between Egypt and Canaan ran along the coast to Beersheba in southern Canaan. This is the most direct route to Hebron where the burial cave is located. The place where they stop to mourn for Jacob is named *Abel-mizraim* (*meadow* or *mourning of Egypt*) by the Canaanites.

Jacob's wishes are fulfilled as he is finally laid to rest in the first land bought by his family in Canaan. The site of this cave, now in the nation of Jordan, is covered by a mosque that is one of the most sacred shrines in Islam. Inside this shrine of the patriarch, six symbolic tombs represent those who are buried there (Abraham, Sarah, Isaac, Rebekah, Jacob, and Leah). A grill set in the floor of the mosque allows pilgrims to gaze into the darkness of the cave below, though nothing may be seen inside the cave itself.

Joseph and the people of Israel return to Egypt. Their stay there is not yet ended.

Verses 15-21: The brothers doubt the sincerity of Joseph's recent goodwill toward them. Though they were reunited with Joseph and welcomed by him, they apparently have not yet confessed their guilt to him and asked his forgiveness. Such confession and forgiveness are necessary before the family members can be truly reconciled with one another.

Joseph's response to them (verses 19-21; see also Genesis 45:7-8) sums up the central message of the whole story: Despite human evil and natural disasters, God is in control of their destiny. God's good purposes for them will be fulfilled.

The Death of Joseph (50:22-26)

Like his father before him, Joseph adopts his grandsons into the covenant family.

Before his death, he passes the blessings and promises given to Abraham, Isaac, and Jacob on to his brothers (and, thus, to their descendants who become the people of Israel). They will be brought out of the land of Egypt in the Exodus (see also Genesis 15:13-14; Exodus 12:51; Hebrews 11:22).

Joseph asks his brothers to swear an oath that they will see that Joseph is eventually buried in Canaan. His body was taken to Canaan four hundred years later, and he was buried at Shechem (see also Exodus 13:19; Joshua 24:32).

§ § § § § § §

The Message of Genesis 48–50

Joseph testifies about the power of God's presence in his life and in the world at large (see Genesis 50:20). This testimony is the fundamental message of the story of Joseph and of the book of Genesis as a whole. In this verse, the Hebrew word that is translated as *meant* in the NRSV can also be translated *intended* or *planned*. Thus Joseph tells us that God plans good for the world, even in the face of human evil. What do Joseph and Genesis tell us about this good?

§ The goodness and blessings of God are built into creation (see, for example, Genesis 1).

§ God remains faithful to the ancient covenant promises, which are passed from one generation of the covenant family to the next (see Genesis 50:24).

§ God brings good out of evil and brings life out of death (see, for example, Genesis 21:5-7; also Psalm 40:5, 17; Romans 8:28).

§ God uses people to help bring about good in the world (see, for example, Genesis 12:1-3; 45:5). This good is part of the fulfillment of God's ultimate purposes for creation and for the community of faith.

§ § § § § § §

Conclusion to Genesis

The book of Genesis shows us that the earth and its creatures exist because of the will and power of God. Likewise, Genesis tells us that the community of faith was born because God desired to have a people with whom to dwell in a mutually fulfilling relationship. This community began when Abraham answered God's call to journey to a new land and to live in a faithful relationship with God (see Genesis 12:1-4). God made a covenant with Abraham (see Genesis 15) to establish this special relationship. The covenant promises were not just for Abraham, however, because God renewed the covenant with Isaac (see Genesis 26:1-5) and with Jacob (see Genesis 28:10-17). The covenant was for both the present and the future, and it was not just for one person but for a whole people. The promises and responsibilities of the covenant were carried forward by each succeeding generation. Abraham was but one man, but through him God sought and eventually gained a faithful community with whom to abide.

The covenant is the foundation of the relationship between God and the community of faith, both in the past and in the present. It is important, then, to understand what the covenant is, how it began, and how it developed both in the Old and the New Testaments.

Covenant in the Old Testament

In general, a covenant is a solemn promise between two partners that is sealed with an oath and/or symbolic action. The Old Testament speaks of different types of covenants, which vary according to the covenant partners and the types of promises made in the covenant agreement. In some cases, the covenant is between two individuals who pledge loyalty and friendship to one another (see, for example, 1 Samuel 18:3; 20:12-17) or who pledge to respect one another's territorial rights (see, for example, Genesis 21:22-24; 26:26-31). Leaders make covenants with groups of people who agree to carry out certain obligations (see, for example, Joshua 24:25; 2 Kings 11:4-8). Even the covenants that may be said to have such secular concerns, however, bind the partners in a sacred obligation because God is called as a witness to the promises made (as in Genesis 31:49-50).

The most important kind of covenant in the Old Testament is that made between God and individuals or between God and a group of people. These sacred covenants are the foundation upon which the community of faith was built. Though we may speak of *the* covenant, there are in fact many covenants made by God in the Old Testament. Each of these covenants was part of the larger covenant relationship that God established with the people of Israel. The primary expression of this covenant relationship is found in the Ten Commandments, but these commandments were only part of the whole covenant process. Beginning in Genesis, the Old Testament shows us how the covenant relationship between God and the chosen people began and how it developed over the centuries. The following Scriptures highlight this process of growth and change:

—Genesis 9:8-17: God makes a covenant with Noah on behalf of all the creatures of the earth for all time. God is responsible for keeping the covenant promises, and humankind has only to accept this gift and to remember and understand the meaning of the sign of the rainbow.

—Genesis 12:1-3: Though the word *covenant* is not used in this text, God and Abraham establish a relationship in

which each has obligations to the other. These promises and obligations are for both the present and the future. God promises Abraham many descendants and great blessings. Abraham must respond with faith and obedience.

—*Genesis 15:5, 18:* In this text we see how the covenant agreement between God and Abraham is formally ratified. Abraham provides the animals for sacrifice and responds in faith to God's promises. God promises Abraham an heir, many descendants, and a homeland.

—*Genesis 17:1-8:* Abraham receives the covenant promises on behalf of his descendants as God establishes an *everlasting covenant* with these future generations. God and people are forever bound to one another.

—*Exodus 6:2-8:* By the time of this Scripture, generations have passed in which Abraham's descendants have become slaves in Egypt, but God has not forgotten the covenant promises. The covenant relationship is renewed when God promises the people of Israel that *I will take you as my people, and I will be your God.*

—*Exodus 19:5-6; 20:1-17:* God declares to Moses that the people of Israel are to be God's special possession or *treasured possession.* The covenant relationship between God and Israel involves responsibilities as well as privileges, however. For the people of God to *keep* the covenant means that they must live righteously before God and obey God's laws. The most distinctive expression of these laws is found in the Ten Commandments. These commandments define the responsibilities of the people toward God and toward one another.

—*Jeremiah 31:31-34:* After many more generations have passed, God reveals to Jeremiah a new development in the covenant relationship. The covenant made in the time of Moses has been broken time and again by the people of Israel. They have worshiped other gods, have been false to one another, and have failed to trust in God. Thus, in future days God will make a new covenant with the chosen people that will be internal instead of external. The covenant laws will be part of their inward nature and not just an external code by which they live. The people's hearts, which are believed to be the wellsprings of human character, will be imprinted with the saving knowledge of God.

The Old Testament tells us that, in the beginning, God called one man and made a covenant with one man. Through Abraham's faith and God's steadfast love a community of faith was born. This community was and is a covenant community, for it was created by and is sustained by God's covenant. Though this covenant has changed through time to serve God's purposes, the basic promise remains the same: *I will be their God, and they shall be my people.* New Testament faith builds on this promise from the Old Testament and looks to the hope and fulfillment of the new covenant.

Covenant in the New Testament

The prophecy of Jeremiah concerning the new covenant had a great influence on the New Testament and on the way the early Christian church carried out the covenant tradition that was their heritage from Old Testament faith. The distinction between the "old" and "new" covenants also influenced the division of Scripture into the Old and New Testaments (that is, Old and New "Covenants").

Jeremiah declared that the new covenant was to be a new saving act by God on behalf of the people of Israel. Israel had not lived up to the old covenant, but their special relationship to God was not completely broken. They were to receive a new covenant based on God's lovingkindness, faithfulness, and justice. This new covenant was to be one of an inward and personal relationship to God. The people of God would have a new heart, engraved with God's statutes, and through this intimate knowledge of God's saving will a new covenant community would be born. According to the New Testament, this new covenant came through the incarnation and revelation of Jesus Christ.

The following Scriptures show how the covenant relationship is fulfilled and recreated in the New Testament:

—*Luke 1:68-75:* Zechariah's prophecy reveals that the coming of the Redeemer is part of God's *holy covenant* and part of God's promises made to Abraham so many years before.

—*Matthew 26:26-28; Mark 14:22-25; Luke 22:17-20:* Jesus declares that his shed blood is the *blood of the* [new] *covenant* (see also 1 Corinthians 11:25; Exodus 24:8). Thus, the new covenant is ratified by the lifeblood of Jesus. The Last Supper is a covenant ceremony in which Christ and his believers are bound to one another. The bread and the cup seal and commemorate this relationship whenever this sacrament is celebrated.

—*John 13:34-35:* Members of the new covenant community live under a new commandment of love for one another. This love is to be a sign to the rest of the world that they are Christ's disciples under the new covenant.

—*2 Corinthians 3:4-6; Galatians 3:15-29:* Paul declares that it is through the Spirit in Jesus Christ that we who come after Abraham may be heirs to God's promises and ministers under the new covenant. The chosen people were unable to live faithfully under the written code, or old covenant, and brought judgment on themselves. God responded with a new saving act, a new covenant of the Spirit in which God's people find new life as the body of Christ.

—*Hebrews 8:6-13; 10:26-36; 12:24; 13:20:* The writer of Hebrews declares that Jesus is the means by which God brings the new covenant to humankind. This new covenant is not just new in time but also new in quality, and it is an eternal covenant. The coming of Jesus with this new covenant fulfills, perfects, and replaces the old covenant. Under the new covenant, believers are to live in faith and hope. They are to encourage one another to follow Jesus' commandment of love and to practice good works in their daily lives. They are to meet together regularly to maintain the covenant community. Above all they are to desire that God's will work in and through them to accomplish that which is pleasing to God through Jesus Christ.

From this brief review of Old and New Testament Scriptures concerning covenant we see that, in each case, the covenant teaches us something about who we are in relation to God and to one another. God is revealed to us through the development of the covenant as a God who seeks a close personal relationship with the covenant people. This revelation shows us what the focus, goals, and boundaries of human existence are supposed to be. From their beginnings in the book of Genesis, the Scriptures show us that the hallmarks of the covenant people are faith, trust, and obedience. All of life is to be understood and lived from the standpoint of God's covenant with us.

Glossary of Terms

Ai: Ancient town approximately two miles southeast of Bethel in the hills north of Jerusalem.

Amalekites: A desert-dwelling nomadic tribe who are the descendants of Amalek, a grandson of Esau.

Amorites: A Semitic people living in parts of Canaan and east of the Jordan River; Jerusalem was probably an Amorite town before the Israelites settled there; descendants of Canaan.

Arabia: A large peninsula in southwest Asia, bordered on the west by the Red Sea and on the east by the Persian Gulf; from a word meaning desert or steppe.

Aram: Land of the Arameans, a Semitic people; an area roughly east of the Jordan River and northeast of Palestine around into the upper Tigris-Euphrates valley.

Ararat: A mountainous region in southeastern Turkey and northwestern Iran.

Assyria: A civilization which, along with Babylonia, flourished in Mesopotamia from approximately 2500–2000 B.C. to its defeat by Babylonia in approximately 612 B.C.

Babylonia: A great civilization of Mesopotamia from approximately 612 B.C. until 539 B.C.

Beersheba: Major city and religious center in the Negeb; often named as the southern limit of the nation of Israel (see, for example, Judges 20:1).

Bethel: Town in the hills north of Jerusalem, founded around 2000 B.C.

Bitumen: Mineral pitch (a mixture of hydrocarbon) or asphalt; used as mortar and as caulking for rafts and basket boats.

Canaan: The territory covering, approximately, Palestine west of the Jordan River and part of western Syria.

Canaanites: The peoples occupying the land of Canaan before the Israelite invasion.

Chaldeans: The people of Chaldea, a region in southern Babylonia; during the reign of King Nebuchadnezzar (604–562 B.C.) Chaldean came to mean *Babylonian.*

Cherubim: Winged creatures who are angelic and spiritual beings, often the guardians of sacred places.

Covenant: A solemn promise between two partners that is sealed with an oath and/or symbolic action. The basic terms of God's covenant with Israel are found in the Ten Commandments (See Exodus 20:1-17; Deuteronomy 5:1-21).

Cubit: A unit for measuring length; the standard cubit is approximately eighteen inches long.

Cush: Biblical name of two territories: (1) land south of Egypt in the present-day Sudan; also called Ethiopia; (2) land of the Kassites in Mesopotamia; also called Cossaea.

Cyprus: An island in the Mediterranean Sea approximately forty miles from Asia Minor and sixty miles from Syria; also called Kittim.

Dan: A son of Jacob and the tribe of his descendants; also a city at the northern limit of Israel.

Egypt: A land in northwest Africa along the Nile River; one of the earliest and most powerful civilizations of the ancient Near East.

Elam: A region east of the Euphrates-Tigris Rivers on the slopes of the Iranian plateau.

Euphrates: One of the major rivers of Mesopotamia; the largest river in western Asia, flowing from Turkey to the Persian Gulf.

Gerar: An important city and district southwest of Canaan near the Mediterranean coast.

Gilead: A hilly region east of the Jordan River between the Sea of Galilee and the Dead Sea, well known for its fertility.

Girgashites: A Canaanite tribe that was among the peoples dispossessed by the Israelites.

Gomorrah: A wicked city destroyed by God along with Sodom, now under the southern part of the Dead Sea.

Hebrews: In the larger sense, the descendants of Eber; more specifically, the Israelite people.

Haran: City in northern Mesopotamia in what is now Turkey, to which Abraham's family migrated on their way from Ur to Canaan.

Hittites: An Indo-European people who were a great power in Asia Minor from approximately 1650–1200 B.C.; later centers of power were in Hamath and northern Syria; also were among the inhabitants of Canaan.

Hivites: One of the native populations of Canaan before the Israelite settlement; also called Horites.

Horites: (1) Name of a people living in the region of Seir before its occupation by the Edomites; (2) also the name of one of the native population groups of Canaan, sometimes called Hivites.

Ishmaelites: Descendants of Ishmael, the son of Abraham by Hagar; identified as nomadic caravan traders.

Jebusites: A clan associated with the Amorites that was in control of Jerusalem before its conquest by David; descendants of Canaan.

Kadmonites: A Semitic people who were nomads or shepherds living in the Syrian Desert between Palestine-Syria and the Euphrates River.

Kassites: People originally from the highlands of present-day Iran who settled parts of the Mesopotamian plain in the 17th–16th centuries B.C.

Kenites: A nomadic or semi-nomadic tribe of metalworkers living generally in southern Judah.

Kenizzites: A people composed of various tribes, including descendants of Caleb, who moved into southern Canaan before the Israelite conquest.

Lud: Son of Shem; the plural form (*Ludim*) may indicate two groups of people, one living in Asia Minor and one in north Africa.

Media: Kingdom of the Medes; an area in northwestern Iran that was first settled in 1400–1000 B.C.

Mesopotamia: The region between the Tigris and Euphrates Rivers, in present-day Iraq.

Midianites: Descendants of Midian, Abraham's son by Keturah; the *land of Midian* was in northwestern Arabia on the eastern shore of the Gulf of Aqabah.

Negeb: Dry region in southern Canaan that runs from the Sinai Peninsula to the Dead Sea; the name sometimes simply means "south."

Nod: Means "wandering"; the land of Cain's exile east of Eden; its exact location is unknown.

Paran: A wilderness area south of Canaan, west of Edom, and north of the wilderness of Sinai.

Perizzites: One of the native population groups in Canaan living in the central highlands; their exact identity is unknown.

Philistia: Home of the Philistines, sea peoples who settled on the southern Mediterranean coast of Palestine in 1200 B.C.

Phoenicia: A group of city-states on the Mediterranean coast in what is now Lebanon; the Phoenicians were great seafarers, explorers, and traders who thrived from approximately 1200–146 B.C.

Rephaim: An ethnic term for the pre-Israelite inhabitants of the Transjordan (land east of the Jordan River).

Seir: The chief mountain range of Edom, south and east of Judah between the Dead Sea and the Gulf of Aqabah, also called Mount Seir.

Semite: Someone who is a descendant of Shem, the son of Noah, or who speaks a Semitic language (for example, Arabs, Arameans, Assyrians, Babylonians, Canaanites, Hebrews, and Phoenicians).

Shechem: Town about forty miles north of Jerusalem, originally Canaanite; became an important Israelite religious and political center.

Shekel: In Old Testament times, a unit of weight (approximately .4 ounces); in New Testament times, a coin of the same weight.

Sodom: A wicked city destroyed by God along with Gomorrah; now under the southern part of the Dead Sea.

Sumer/Sumerians: A region in southern Mesopotamia between present-day Bagdad and the Persian Gulf; the Sumerian civilization flourished between 3300 and 1700 B.C. and was the earliest known society where people could read and write.

Tigris: One of the major rivers of Mesopotamia; flows from the mountains of Turkey and Iraq over 1,000 miles to the Persian Gulf.

Unleavened bread: Bread or cakes baked without yeast.

Ur: Ancient city on the Euphrates River in southern Mesopotamia in present-day Iraq; home of Abraham.

Zoar: Town on the southeastern side of the Dead Sea basin; name means *little*.

Guide to Pronunciation

Abimelech: Ah-BIH-meh-leck
Ai: EYE
Amalek: AM-ah-lek
Aram: AIR-um
Ararat: AIR-ah-rat
Arameans: Air-ah-MEE-ans
Arpachshad: Ar-POCK-shad
Atad: AY-tad
Beer-la-hai-roi: BEER-lah-HIGH-roi
Beersheba: Beer-SHEH-bah
Berith: Buh-REETH
Bethuel: BETH-you-ell
Bilhah: BILL-hah
Canaan: KAY-nun
Chaldeans: Kal-DEE-ans
Cherubim: CHER-uh-bim
Cush: KOOSH
Dothan: DOH-thun
Eder: AY-der
Edom: EE-dum
Elam: EE-lum
Eliezer: Eh-leeh-AY-zer
Eliphaz: EH-lih-faz
Elohim: Eh-loh-HEEM
Elohist: EH-loh-hist
Elyon: Eh-lee-ON

Enoch: EE-nuck
Enosh: EE-nosh
Ephraim: EE-frah-eem
Ephron: EFF-ron
Euphrates: You-FRAY-tees
Gerar: Ger-ARE
Gerizim: Geh-rih-ZEEM
Gezer: GEH-zer
Gihon: GEE-hon
Goshen: GOH-shen
Hagar: HAY-gar
Hamor: Hah-MORE
Haran: Hah-RAHN
Havilah: HAV-ih-lah
Hazor: Hah-TSORE
Hebron: HEH-brun
Hivites: HIH-vites
Idumeans: Ih-doo-ME-ans
Irad: EAR-rad
Ishmael: ISH-may-ell
Issachar: IS-ah-kahr
Jabal: JAY-bal
Japheth: JAH-feth
Jared: JAR-ed
Jebusites: JEB-you-sites
Jubel: JOO-bal
Kadesh: KAY-desh
Kenan: KEN-an
Kenites: KEN-ites
Keturah: Keh-TURE-ah
Laban: LAY-ban
Lamech: LAH-meck
Lud: LOOD
Machpelah: Mahk-peh-LAH
Mahalalel: Mah-HAH-luh-lel
Mahalath: Mah-hah-LATH
Mahanaim: Mah-hah-NAH-yim

Mamre: MAM-reh
Media: MEE-dee-ah
Mehujael: Meh-HOO-jah-el
Melchizedek: Mel-KIZ-eh-deck
Mesopotamia: Meh-soh-poh-TAME-ee-ah
Methuselah: Meh-THOO-zeh-lah
Methushael: Meh-THOO-shah-el
Midianites: MIH-dee-ah-nites
Milcah: MIL-kah
Moab: MOH-ab
Moriah: Moh-RIGH-ah
Naamah: NAY-ah-mah
Nahor: NAY-hor
Naphtali: NAFF-tah-lee
Negeb: NEH-geb
Nephilim: Neh-fih-LEEM
Onan: OH-nan
Paddan-aram: PAD-an-AIR-em
Peleg: PAY-leg
Peniel: PEH-nee-el
Pentateuch: PEN-tah-tuke
Penuel: PEN-you-el
Pharaoh: FAIR-oh
Phicol: FIGH-col
Philistines: FILL-iss-teens
Phoenicia: Foh-NEE-shah
Pishon: PIE-shon
Potiphar: POH-tih-far
Potiphera: Poh-TIH-fuh-ruh
Put: POOT
Rameses: RAM-sees
Rephaim: REH-fah-yim
Sarah: SAIR-ah
Sarai: Sah-RIGH
Shaddai: Shah-DIGH
Shechem: SHECK-em
Shelah: Sheh-LAH

Sheol: Sheh-OLE
Shinar: SHIGH-nar
Simeon: SIH-mee-un
Succoth: SUH-kuth
Sumer: SOO-mer
Tamar: TAY-mar
Terah: TER-ah
Tigris: TIGH-gris
Tubal-Cain: TOO-ball-CAIN
Yahweh: YAH-way
Yahwist: YAH-wist
Zadok: ZAY-dock
Zebulun: ZEB-you-lun
Zilpah: ZIL-pah

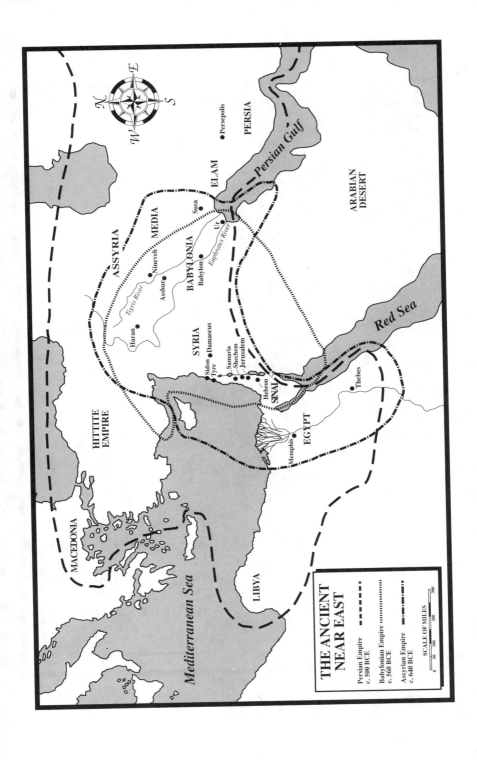

THE ANCIENT
NEAR EAST

Persian Empire
c. 500 BCE

Babylonian Empire
c. 560 BCE

Assyrian Empire
c. 640 BCE

SCALE OF MILES

0   50   100   200   300

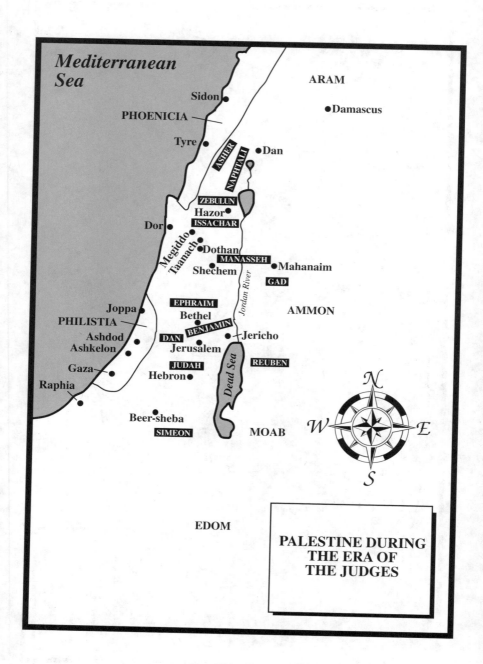

Mediterranean Sea

ARAM

●Damascus

Sidon

PHOENICIA

Tyre

ASHER
NAPHTALI ●Dan

ZEBULUN
Hazor●
ISSACHAR

Dor●

Megiddo
Taanach ●Dothan
MANASSEH ●Mahanaim
Shechem
GAD

Joppa
PHILISTIA
EPHRAIM
Bethel
BENJAMIN
Ashdod DAN ●Jericho
Ashkelon Jerusalem

AMMON

Jordan River

Gaza
JUDAH
Hebron●

Dead Sea

REUBEN

Raphia

Beer-sheba●
SIMEON MOAB

EDOM

N
W E
S

PALESTINE DURING
THE ERA OF
THE JUDGES